Scarlett Johansson

Hollywood Superstar

Michael A. Schuman

Enslow Publishers, Inc.
40 Industrial Road
Box 398
Berkeley Heights, NJ 07922
USA

http://www.enslow.com

Library of Congress Cataloging-in-Publication Data

Schuman, Michael.

    Scarlett Johansson : Hollywood superstar / Michael A. Schuman.

        p. cm. — (People to know today)

    Summary: "A biography of American actress Scarlett Johansson"—Provided by publisher.

    Includes bibliographical references and index.

    Includes filmography and webliography.

    ISBN 978-0-7660-3556-0

    1. Johansson, Scarlett, 1984- Juvenile literature. 2. Actors—United States—Biography—Juvenile literature. I. Title.

    PN2287.J575S575 2010

    791.430'28092—dc22

    [B]

2010010279

Printed in the United States of America

122010 Lake Book Manufacturing, Inc., Melrose Park, IL

10 9 8 7 6 5 4 3 2 1

To Our Readers: This book is not authorized by Scarlett Johansson.

We have done our best to make sure all Internet addresses in this book were active and appropriate when we went to press. However, the author and publisher have no control over and assume no liability for the material available on those Internet sites or on other Web sites they may link to. Any comments or suggestions can be sent by e-mail to comments@enslow.com or to the address on the back cover.

♻ Enslow Publishers, Inc., is committed to printing our books on recycled paper. The paper in every book contains 10% to 30% post-consumer waste (PCW). The cover board on the outside of each book contains 100% PCW. Our goal is to do our part to help young people and the environment too!

Photos and Illustrations: Alex Berliner/BEImages/Rex USA, p. 12; Associated Press, pp. 1, 4, 89; © Buena Vista/courtesy Everett Collection, p. 7; courtesy Everett Collection, p. 13; Dan Steinberg/BEImages/Rex USA, p. 10; Dee Cercone/Everett Collection, p. 85; © DreamWorks/courtesy Everett Collection, p. 67; © Focus Features/courtesy Everett Collection, pp. 47, 83; Gregorio T. Binuya/Everett Collection, p. 90; © Lions Gate/courtesy Everett Collection, p. 57; © Orion/courtesy Everett Collection, p. 16; © Sony Pictures Classics/courtesy Everett Collection, p. 25; Starstock/Photoshot/Everett Collection B89_053128, p. 32; © United Artists/courtesy Everett Collection, p. 38; © Universal/courtesy Everett Collection, p. 73; © USA Films/courtesy Everett Collection, p. 35; © Warner Brothers. Courtesy Everett Collection, p. 44; © Weinstein Company/Courtesy Everett Collection, p. 81.

Cover Illustration: Associated Press (Scarlett Johansson from the shoulders up).

CONTENTS

Scarlett Johansson

1
NOT JUST HORSING AROUND

Scarlett Johansson had been acting in movies since she was eight. But she was hardly famous. Scarlett was like any other child actor. She appeared in films, but her name was unknown outside of the entertainment industry.

Then when she was twelve, she received a special opportunity. A movie titled *The Horse Whisperer* was about to be made. It was based on a book about a man who has an unusual way of healing horses. Instead of treating them roughly, he is gentle with them.

One of the main characters in the movie is Grace MacLean, a young girl who loses a leg in a horseback riding accident. The movie's director, Robert Redford, had plans to cast rising teenage star Natalie Portman to play the role. However, the making of the movie was behind schedule. Portman made other commitments and could no longer play the part. So Redford had to find someone else to play Grace.

He asked young female actors to send in audition tapes. After the tough task of looking through thousands, Redford selected Scarlett for the role.[1] Redford said that Scarlett showed some real emotion in her audition. He admitted, "A lot of young girls just didn't understand that Grace needed a certain depth of spirit."[2]

But for Scarlett, the hard work had just begun. The twelve-year-old took a great deal of time to research the lives of amputees. She spent hours reading true stories about amputees who went on to play sports, including horseback riding. If she was not reading books about amputees' life stories, she watched videos telling their tales. She then met a boy who lost a leg. He showed her how he used his one leg to walk up and down stairs.

Her work paid off. *The Horse Whisperer* was released on May 15, 1998. Most critics liked the movie.[3] In addition, it drew audiences to their neighborhood theaters. The movie earned over $75 million in the United States and over $111 million in foreign countries.[4]

In addition to directing *The Horse Whisperer*, Redford played a lead role in it. The movie also starred established actors Kristin Scott-Thomas and Sam Neill. Yet, it was the little-known twelve-year-old girl who

Scarlett Johansson as thirteen-year-old Grace MacLean in 1998's critically acclaimed *The Horse Whisperer*.

seemed to stand out. One critic, James Berardinelli, mentioned the Academy Awards, or Oscars, in his review. The Oscars are awarded every year to the best movies and the talented people who work on them. He wrote: "There is an Oscar-caliber performance in *The Horse Whisperer*, but it isn't given by Redford, Scott-Thomas, or Neill. Instead, it's the work of young Scarlett Johansson. . . . She does everything necessary to make Grace a living and vital character, and, like all good performers, much of her acting comes through subtle expression changes and body language."[5]

Although Scarlett was not nominated for an Oscar, she did win a Young Star Award. Those are given to the best actors between ages six and eighteen working in movies, television, live stage, or music. Scarlett won best performance by a young actress in a drama film.

More importantly, she earned respect. She would no longer be just another child actor. Graciously, Scarlett gave much of the credit for her performance to Robert Redford. Johansson said, "Robert was incredible to me. He talked to me like I was an adult. I don't think I've ever been so carefully directed by someone. Things always work out for the [right] reason. My career took a different turn."[6]

2

"I WANTED TO BE JUDY GARLAND"

Scarlett Johansson was born just minutes before her twin brother on November 22, 1984, in New York City. Her twin brother is named Hunter. She has an older sister named Vanessa and an older brother named Adrian. She also has an older half brother, Christian, from her father's first marriage.

Scarlett's father, Karsten Johansson, is a Danish-born architect. Perhaps Scarlett received her flair for show business from her grandfather, Ejner Johansson, who was a screenwriter and director in Denmark.

Scarlett's mother, Melanie, is a Jewish woman of eastern European descent. She was born and raised in the Bronx, a borough of New York City. Melanie met Karsten in Denmark, where her mother lived for a short time. Melanie's mother, Dorothy (Scarlett's grandmother), loved

Scarlett Johansson and her twin brother, Hunter, attend a post-Golden Globe Awards party in Los Angeles, California, January 16, 2005.

to sing and dance. She said she had the lead role in every school play in elementary school. Maybe some of Scarlett's talent also came from her grandmother.

There is a rumor among Scarlett's fans that she was named after Scarlett O'Hara from *Gone With the Wind*, a novel about the Civil War. It was made into a movie in 1939 and is regarded by critics as one of the best of all time. The rumor may have sprung from the fact that another important character in *Gone With the Wind* is named Melanie—just like Scarlett's mother. However, Melanie simply liked the name Scarlett. In fact, Melanie almost did not name her daughter Scarlett because she did not want people to think she was named after Scarlett O'Hara.[1]

The Johanssons did not have much money. Government programs paid in part for the Johansson children's school lunches.[2] She remembered, "We were a single-income family with four kids living in New York City. My parents tried not to make a big deal of it, but I know it was a struggle for them."[3]

Though they did not have many material objects, the Johanssons did try to spend as much time together as a family as possible. They celebrated Jewish holidays like Hanukkah and loved going to the movies together.

Melanie especially liked taking Scarlett to see splashy musicals from the 1940s and 1950s. One of these was *Meet Me in St. Louis*, released in 1944. The movie is about four sisters who live in St. Louis in 1904 when the city is hosting a world's fair. Judy Garland, who starred in *The Wizard of Oz* just four years earlier, played the lead in *Meet Me in St. Louis*. Garland sang several popular songs in the movie, including "Have Yourself a Merry Little Christmas." It is a song still heard every holiday season.

Scarlett said, "I was one of those kids who used to stare in the mirror until I made myself cry. I wanted to be Judy Garland in *Meet Me in St. Louis*."[4]

Scarlett poses with her mother, Melanie, in 2003.

Scarlett also spent many hours of her childhood with her grandmother, Dorothy. Dorothy said, "I spent a lot of time with Scarlett when she was younger. People would ask her, 'Who's your best friend?' And she would say, 'Grandma!'"[5]

Like her grandmother, Scarlett loved to give people a show. "I was like a singing, dancing fool," Scarlett said, laughing. She charged her parents and siblings a dollar each to see her do a song and dance routine at home.[6] She explained further, "I actually started

Judy Garland (center) performs a dance number with Margaret O'Brien in the 1944 musical *Meet Me in St. Louis*. Scarlett Johansson greatly admired Judy Garland growing up and wished to be just like her.

acting because I wanted to be in musicals when I was a little girl."[7]

Scarlett and her twin brother, Hunter, began elementary school at P.S. 41, or Public School 41, in the Greenwich Village section of New York City. Many public schools in New York City have numbers as their names. Even in school, Scarlett liked to show off. Her mother realized her daughter had a passion for entertaining and started taking her to auditions for television commercials. Melanie also took Scarlett's brother Adrian to the auditions.

Unfortunately, hardly anyone was interested in Scarlett. Part of the problem was her low voice. She would read her lines and directors would often ask her if she had a cold. They did not think her voice seemed natural for a little girl. Scarlett hated the rejection and often acted out. She conceded, "I had these huge temper tantrums."[8]

What made matters worse was that some commercial directors wanted to hire a different Johansson. She recalled, "The only person they wanted was my older brother who couldn't care less, and who never ended up doing anything."[9]

After one rejection, Scarlett ranted as if she had hit rock bottom. She said, "I was, like, devastated. I decided at that very moment that my whole life was going down the tubes. And my mom was, like: I didn't know you were that interested. And I was, like: yes, yes! How could you not recognize this in me?"[10]

Being rejected may have been hard on Scarlett, but her tantrums were doubly hard on Scarlett's mother, who went out of her way to take the young girl to auditions. Scarlett remembered the whole experience as truly unpleasant. She said, "It was like being in a beauty pageant. The other moms were really scary, and it was awful, a really sordid scene. So I'd throw tantrums and my mom was, like: I don't want to do this anymore! And then I was, like: you can't take this away from me! She was, like: fine, but I'm not going out on these commercials."[11]

Wanting her daughter to be happy, Melanie ditched the idea of television commercials. Since Melanie loved movies, she thought Scarlett might want to try her chance with films. But Melanie wanted Scarlett to have a role model. She had the perfect person in mind.

Jodie Foster is a respected actor, movie producer, and director today. She was born in 1962 and has been acting since she was three. Unlike Scarlett, Foster had success in television commercials. Foster moved from commercials to television programs. She did not star in any that became hits, but she was a guest actor on many. Foster then made several movies for Walt Disney Studios. She starred in the original movie *Freaky Friday* in 1975. Lindsay Lohan played the same role in the 2003 *Freaky Friday* remake.

Many child actors have trouble becoming successful as adult actors. Audiences tend to remember them as children and find it hard to accept them as adults. Some child actors cope by escaping into substance abuse. Foster never had that problem nor has she ever been involved in a public scandal. She has won two Academy Awards for her acting.

Melanie took Scarlett to one of Foster's movies to introduce her to her work. Surprisingly, Melanie showed Scarlett the movie *Silence of the Lambs*. Foster won one of her two Academy Awards for her role in that movie. She plays a young Federal Bureau of Investigation (FBI) agent. However, *Silence of the Lambs* is a movie about a grisly murder. Most children would find the movie disturbing and difficult to watch. But Scarlett handled it well. She admired Foster's acting and wanted to be like her. Watching the movie also made her think about how movies are made.

Jodie Foster as FBI agent Clarice Starling in 1991's thriller *Silence of the Lambs*. Scarlett's mother thought the Academy Award-winning actress would make a good role model for her daughter.

Melanie began taking Scarlett to movie auditions. Although she was just seven, Scarlett was mature for her age. Scarlett felt that commercial directors merely wanted a child with a certain look. In movies, Scarlett stated, "I felt like they weren't casting me because I had long, blonde hair. They were casting me because I had something to offer."[12]

Her throaty voice was not a problem as it had been in commercial auditions. In commercials, her job would be to sell a product. It did not matter if it was cookies, laundry detergent, cars, or life insurance. Companies did not want a little girl with an unusual voice to represent their products. They wanted a child that customers could relate to. But in movies, her job would be to play a character. In film, Scarlett's voice made her seem quirky and colorful.

In 1993, Melanie enrolled Scarlett in a special school in New York City called the Lee Strasberg Theatre Institute for Young People. Strasberg was a much-admired acting teacher for both adults and children.

Strasberg taught an acting style called "method acting." In method acting, actors do not simply play a role. In a way, they try as much as possible to become their character. They try to feel the emotions their characters would feel. Sometimes as part of their training, actors are asked to relive a horrible experience they had in their past. The idea behind that is to help them understand some pain their character may be going through. Even when they are not playing their role, some method actors try to stay in character. Some of the world's greatest actors sharpened their talents at the Strasberg Institute.

Judd Nelson, who acted in the classic teen movie *The Breakfast Club*, is a method actor. His character in that movie was a tough kid from a broken home who was always getting detentions. His character and the one played by Molly Ringwald did not get along. Yet even on breaks between filming, Nelson said he was mean to Ringwald because he did not want to break out of character. Other well-known actors who studied with Lee Strasberg include Marilyn Monroe, Paul Newman, Al Pacino, James Dean, and Robert De Niro.

One would think that would be intense for an eight-year-old. In addition, Scarlett was the youngest in her class.[13] But she was determined and ambitious. After just a half semester, Scarlett was promoted into the "young adult" category of classes.

It did not take long for Scarlett to succeed in artistic acting where she failed in commercials. At age eight, Scarlett landed a part in a play titled *Sophistry*. It was about a violent crime that occurred on a college campus. *Sophistry* was performed on an off-Broadway stage in New York City. The street Broadway has always been the heart of New York City's famed theater district. Off-Broadway does not simply mean that the theater was not on the street Broadway. It refers to the size of the theater—smaller than those for mainstream Broadway plays. Scarlett had only two lines but had to say them every night in front of a live audience. One of her costars was up-and-coming actor Ethan Hawke.

Scarlett kept up her schooling, and it was not before long that she was able to fulfill one of her dreams—to act in a movie.

3
PLAYING MANNY AND MOLLY

The movie was called *North*. It seemed to have a lot going for it. Its director was the respected Rob Reiner. His movies include *Stand By Me, A Few Good Men,* and *When Harry Met Sally.* Some movies are loved by critics but do not draw audiences and lose money. Others are big hits with audiences but critics cannot stand them. Those movies earn money but not respect. Many of Reiner's movies are both loved by critics and draw big audiences.

"North" is the name of both the movie and the title character, a young boy. His parents are successful, but North feels they neglect him by spending too much time working. He feels he is worthy of better parents. North sues his parents in a court and a judge agrees with him. The judge allows North to look for better parents who want to adopt him. If North fails within two months he must return home.

North features an attractive cast. North is played by Elijah Wood, who later starred in the *Lord of the Rings* movies. Bruce Willis narrates the movie. North's parents are played by Jason Alexander and Julia Louis-Dreyfus, who at the time were starring in the hit television comedy *Seinfeld*. Scarlett plays Laura Nelson, the kid sister in a family that wants to adopt North.

Scarlett said that even though she was just a child, she felt very natural playing her part in *North*. She said that "for some reason, I just knew what to do, instinctively. It was like, I don't know . . . fate. I just love everything about making movies."[1]

North came out in the summer of 1994, when Scarlett was nine. Although Reiner had succeeded before, this time his luck changed. Audiences did not go to see *North* and nearly every critic hated it. One of the world's most famous movie critics, Roger Ebert, made his views more than clear. He wrote: "I hated this movie. Hated hated hated hated hated this movie. Hated it. Hated every simpering stupid vacant audience-insulting moment of it."[2]

Sometimes a disastrous movie can harm an actor's career. Movie producers may not want to take a chance on an actor whose last movie was a failure. That can especially happen when a movie is given a lot of publicity. Luckily for Rob Reiner and the cast of *North*, that was not the case here. *North* disappeared from the theaters in a flash and quickly went to home video. However, Scarlett's few minutes on screen did get her noticed by others in the movie industry.

Almost immediately, she was signed to appear in another movie. This time, it was the crime drama *Just Cause,* released in 1995. Scarlett plays the daughter of a law professor who investigates a Florida murder. At one point, Scarlett shows her true skills when the killer threatens her character.

The law professor is played by Scottish actor Sean Connery. Connery is best known for playing spy James Bond in the 1960s. A supporting actor in *Just Cause* is the well-respected Laurence Fishburne. Johansson said she learned a lot from both acting veterans. On one occasion, Fishburne asked Scarlett if she wanted to be an actress or a movie star. Fishburne was basically asking Scarlett if she wanted to act just to become famous, or if she wanted to act because acting is an art. She has said that she has kept Fishburne's question in mind many times since.

Like *North, Just Cause* was not a hit. It was quickly forgotten. On the one hand, more critics liked *Just Cause* than *North*. Still, the majority did not give the movie good reviews. Hal Hinson of the *Washington Post* wrote: "The picture builds to an action-packed climax but, both in terms of story and theme, it never really comes to a satisfying resolution. The longer you stay with it, the more routine and uninspired it seems."[3]

Since Scarlett's role was fairly small and because she was so young, a second failed movie did not hurt her career. She actually got her first television acting role at the age of nine. Scarlett appeared in a skit on the television program, *Late Night With Conan O'Brien.* At the time the show aired from 12:30 A.M. until 1:30 A.M. She appeared unbilled, which means her name was not listed as a cast member. And she was on screen for just a short time. But it was a start. It is interesting that the show aired too late for most children to watch it.

But Scarlett's future was not in television. She kept getting movie roles. Her next movie, *If Lucy Fell,* came out in the spring of 1996 when Scarlett was eleven. It was a different type of movie for Scarlett. For one thing, it was a romantic comedy. *If Lucy Fell* is a bittersweet story. It brings out feelings of both sadness and hope. The leads are played by Sarah Jessica Parker and Eric Schaeffer.

The plot is a far-fetched story of two desperate people. Lucy (Parker) and Joe (Schaeffer) are roommates and best friends. Lucy is a therapist and Joe is an artist and teacher. Both are nearing their thirtieth birthdays. They once jokingly made a pact that if they did not find true love by the time they reached thirty they would jump off the Brooklyn Bridge together.

Now both have become so desperate they consider taking the pact seriously. The movie follows the two as they try to find true love.

If Lucy Fell was Scarlett's first movie in which she did not play someone's daughter. Her role was Emily, one of Joe's smartest students. One thing was not different. *If Lucy Fell* also failed. Unlike *North*, *If Lucy Fell* did wow some critics. Christopher Null of the Web site Filmcritic.com wrote that the movie provided him with "nonstop laughs for a solid 50 minutes."[4]

More typical was the review by James Berardinelli of the Web site Reelviews. He wrote: "For the most part, *If Lucy Fell* is a disappointingly superficial romantic comedy. There's no chemistry between any of the characters. The acting is mediocre, with Schaeffer and Parker exhibiting no screen presence."[5]

Even though Scarlett's parts in her first movies were small, they took a great deal of time to film. A movie director can spend hours setting up and filming a scene that will take up just a minute or two in a movie. That meant that Scarlett had private teachers give her lessons on the movie sets. True, Scarlett was at a special school for children who wanted to be actors. However, she still had to learn basic subjects such as math and history.

About this time, Scarlett's mother also became her manager. A manager's job is to help a performer advance his or her career. Even though Melanie had no professional show-business experience, she had been shuttling Scarlett to one audition after another for years. So Melanie got to know casting agents and other people in the entertainment business. Besides, Melanie always did love the movies. And she is a very determined person.

Scarlett said of her mother, "She's good at getting what she wants. The squeaky wheel gets the grease. That totally describes my mom. We've utilized every resource we've had since I was eight years old to try and think of ways to get things done."[6]

Almost all of Scarlett's immediate family appeared in her next movie, *Manny and Lo*. Her parents, sister,

Aleska Palladino and eleven-year-old Scarlett costar in the 1996 independent film *Manny and Lo*.

Vanessa, and brother Hunter all had small parts. But Scarlett, at just eleven years old, was a costar. For the first time, she was not lost in the background behind older and more well-established actors. That meant more responsibility. If the movie failed, she might not get a free pass as she had gotten in her past films.

Writer and director Lisa Krueger had never directed a film before. In addition, *Manny and Lo* was not made by a big, established production company. *Manny and Lo* is known in the entertainment business as an independent movie. Big studios have professional publicity departments that promote their movies. Krueger did not have that luxury. Instead of big multiplexes, *Manny and Lo* was shown mostly in single theaters specializing in independent or foreign movies.

The story of *Manny and Lo* is simple. Amanda, or Manny, is played by Scarlett. She is an eleven-year-old girl who grew up in an abusive home with her sixteen-year-old sister, Laurel, or Lo. Lo is played by Aleska Palladino. The sisters then live in a series of foster homes but are never treated well. Finally, the girls run away. The movie follows them as they make their way on their own.

Manny and Lo is narrated by Scarlett, in character as Manny. Her smoky voice that did not work well in commercials works perfectly in this movie. Unlike the movies Scarlett had appeared in earlier, *Manny and Lo* was mostly loved by movie critics. Plenty of them had special words or praise for Scarlett's acting ability.

Barbara Shulgasser of the *San Francisco Examiner* raved, "*Manny & Lo* grows on you, largely because of the charm of its youngest cast member, Scarlett Johansson, who plays 11-years-old Amanda."[7] Shulgasser added, "Johansson is a wonderful, natural actress. She is never cloying; she conveys Manny's defiance in a muted and surprisingly dignified manner. She's also funny."[8]

James Berardinelli of the Reelviews Web site said of Scarlett: "She was tremendous in *Manny & Lo*. I wrote at the time that she is an actress to watch."[9] Berardinelli also wrote that Scarlett's portrayal of "Manny is so perfectly on-target that, while watching her, it's easy to forget that this is an actress playing a role.[10]

About this time, Scarlett finished her studies at the Strasberg Institute. She transferred to the Professional Children's School (PCS). PCS was founded in 1914 as a private school for children who worked as actors.

Because of their work schedules, child actors can not usually attend regular public schools. So many children who graduated from PCS became professional actors that by the 1930s it was known as Broadway's little red schoolhouse—even though classes were taught in a skyscraper. Current actors who attended PCS include Macaulay Culkin, Uma Thurman, Donald Faison, Jane Krakowski, and Ashley Tisdale.

Scarlett was honored with her first award nomination for her work in *Manny and Lo*. It was for an Independent Spirit Award in the category of best lead female. The Independent Spirit Awards are devoted to movies made by independent filmmakers. For a long time, independent movies were ignored by the famous Academy Awards. However, that pattern has changed a bit in recent years.

Scarlett did not win. The award went to Frances McDormand, who played a sheriff in the offbeat crime comedy/drama *Fargo*. Nevertheless, it was a special honor to be nominated for best actress at just eleven years old.

Manny and Lo had made its debut at the Sundance Film Festival in 1996. This festival takes place every year at a resort in Utah. It showcases movies made by independents, not by the big studios. Other types of movies presented at Sundance include foreign films, documentaries, and short films. If it was not for festivals such as Sundance Film Festival, such movies would be not likely to receive any publicity at all.

One of the founders of the Sundance Film Festival is actor and director Robert Redford. After Redford viewed Scarlett's acting performance in *Manny and Lo*, he made the decision to cast her in the movie, *The Horse Whisperer*.[11] Before *The Horse Whisperer* was released in 1998, however, Scarlett had roles in two more movies.

One, released in 1997, was titled *Fall.* Like *If Lucy Fell,* it was also a dark, romantic comedy. Scarlett had a very small role. Her character was not even named. She was credited merely as "Little Girl." Her next movie, which also came out in 1997, was *Home Alone 3.* It was the third of four movies in the popular *Home Alone* series. It was also the first *Home Alone* movie that did not star Macauley Culkin, who was by then too old to play the lead.

This version of *Home Alone* starred Alex D. Linz, who plays eight-year-old Alex Pruitt. Thirteen-year-old Scarlett plays his big sister, Molly. As in the first two *Home Alone* movies, there is a lot of slapstick violence, and the little kid always outsmarts the bad guys in the end. Most critics thought it was merely a rehash of the first two *Home Alone* movies but with a different cast. However, it did make a profit in theaters.[12] It was the first movie Scarlett made for a kids' audience since *North.*

Scarlett auditioned for the lead in an upcoming Disney Studio movie. It was a remake of the 1961 comedy smash *The Parent Trap.* However, that role went to another young actor, Lindsay Lohan. Then in 1998 Scarlett's breakout movie, *The Horse Whisperer,* was released. Suddenly the thirteen-year-old was famous.

4

SCARLETT THE STARLET

Since Scarlett Johansson had a successful movie behind her, some might think her future in the movies was all brightness and sunshine—that she would ever have to work hard to get a good role again. But in the wake of *The Horse Whisperer*, Scarlett seemed to be offered just one kind of role—that of a victimized girl. She said, "After I did *The Horse Whisperer*, I got a whole slew of scripts about girls who were getting raped and cut into little pieces; or, you know, girls who were horseback-riding champions who then got some fatal disease, all these Cinderella stories, or heartbreaking stories, or disgusting slayer stories."[1]

Because she excelled in her role as Grace MacLean, Scarlett was in danger of being typecast, or given the same type of role over and over. Since actors are often lucky to get movie offers, some do not mind being typecast. They are happy to get the work.

Scarlett's mother and manager, Melanie, did not want to take the chance of her daughter being typecast. She suggested that Scarlett bide her time and wait for a different type of role. Melanie fired agents who tried to pressure Scarlett into taking roles she did not like. Scarlett did not mince words when discussing those agents. She remarked, "I was like, 'Obviously, you don't understand me, or what I'm about, so why are we working together?'"[2]

It helped that Scarlett was still a child. She did not have the financial obligations adults have. Scarlett explained, "And because I wasn't supporting anybody, like I wasn't supporting my family, I was just able to do whatever I wanted to do."[3]

However, that did not mean that Scarlett did not have difficulties in her family life. Her parents' marriage had been crumbling for a while. Finally, they divorced.

Scarlett took this abrupt change in her life in a very mature and professional manner. She said, "I'm not a 'poor me' kind of person. Certain cards were dealt to me, and I had to be strong. My parents divorced when I was 13. The actual separation wasn't hard, but things that come with divorce are difficult. But those things mold you to be the person that you are. I've always been very determined, ever since I was a little girl, to

This photograph of a young Scarlett Johansson was taken April 21, 1998, the same year her breakthrough movie *The Horse Whisperer* was released.

make my way. And I am also very responsible. It's just who I am."[4]

As far as movie roles, Melanie and Scarlett's patience paid off. Different offers did come along. Her next movie was the opposite of *The Horse Whisperer*. It was a silly romp titled *My Brother the Pig*. Scarlett had the lead role as fourteen-year-old Kathy Caldwell. Kathy has a younger brother named George whose favorite hobby seems to be pestering Kathy. She just wants him to disappear.

When Kathy and George's parents go on vacation, Kathy gets her wish. George is put under a spell after making contact with a babysitter's magic rocks. George may have acted like a pig to his sister in the past, but the spell turns him into a real pig. Kathy, her babysitter, and a few other people learn that the antidote to the spell is known only by the babysitter's grandmother in Mexico. So they travel to Mexico to try to reverse it before Kathy's parents return.

While Scarlett got her wish by acting in a movie different from *The Horse Whisperer*, *My Brother the Pig* was not successful. Movie critics Mick Martin and Marsha Porter gave the movie a moderately acceptable rating, mainly because of Scarlett's appearance. In their review, they refer to the fact that, in France, pigs are used to root out wild truffles, mushrooms that are delicacies. They wrote: "Family film doesn't turn up any truffles, but it's serviceable as a springboard for up-and-coming talent."[5] *My Brother the Pig* did not play long in the theaters and was soon forgotten.

Scarlett was given a more serious role in her next film, *The Man Who Wasn't There*. Like *The Horse Whisperer*, *The Man Who Wasn't There* had a respected and established director, Joel Coen. Joel and his brother, Ethan, had for years directed movies that tended to be dark and offbeat.

Scarlett had a small role in *The Man Who Wasn't There*, but it was an important one. The movie takes place in Santa Rosa, California, in 1949. Coen did not make *The Man Who Wasn't There* in a typical manner. He shot the movie in color. Then, to fit the period, he used high technology to print it in black and white.

So people in theaters saw it in black and white. The genre is called film noir, or "black film" in French. It was popular in the 1940s and early 1950s. The subject matter of film noir is usually crime, and the characters are often shady.

In *The Man Who Wasn't There*, actor Billy Bob Thornton plays Ed Crane, a barber who runs his own business. Since he needs money, he decides to black-mail another man. At one point in the movie, Ed murders the man, causing numerous complications in the plot.

Scarlett plays a talented teenage classical piano player named Rachael "Birdy" Abundas. Although Birdie is half Ed's age, Ed finds himself romantically attracted to Birdie. Scarlett, as Birdie, appears in late 1940s-era clothing and sports a mousy brown hairstyle.

The Man Who Wasn't There received great reviews. One of the few critics who did not like it was Todd McCarthy who writes for the show-business publication *Variety*. Still, he gave a tip of the hat to Scarlett for her performance. McCarthy wrote that she is "much grown since *The Horse Whisperer* and very good."[6]

Although Scarlett was just a teenager and little experienced compared to Joel Coen, she did not lack in confidence. That even meant rejecting Coen's ideas if she did not like them—even though Coen was in charge. Her costar, Billy Bob Thornton, recalled that at one point Coen suggested that Birdy eat sunflower seeds during a scene. Thornton remembered, "She said, 'Why would I eat sunflower seeds?' She looked at Joel like, 'You idiot. What are you talking about?' Joel was like, 'I'm sorry.' And slinked out of the room."[7]

Joel Coen confessed, "I think we were all a little intimidated by Scarlett."[8] Thornton added, "Most people have self-doubt at some point in their lives or work. Scarlett doesn't have that."[9]

Unlike many teenage actors, Scarlett continued to appear in offbeat films. Her next movie, *Ghost World*, was based on a book of the same name written in the form of a graphic novel. A graphic novel is a story—usually an unconventional one—told in comic-book form.

Scarlett as Rachael "Birdy" Abundas in *The Man Who Wasn't There*.

Ghost World was directed by Terry Zwigoff. Zwigoff took a risk making a graphic novel into a movie. Many movies based on comics or video games are thought little of by critics and do not make money.

Zwigoff knew that *Ghost World* required actors who had worked in unusual films. Scarlett Johansson was the perfect choice to play one of the two leads. Cast in the other lead was Thora Birch. In 1999, Birch costarred in the Academy Award-winning movie *American Beauty*. Birch played the teenage daughter in an unhappy family.

In *Ghost World*, Johansson and Birch play pessimistic teenagers Rebecca and Enid. Enid is the main character and Rebecca is her sidekick. In the movie's beginning, the two just graduated high school. They form a friendship because they are different from most teenagers in their town. They think their fellow teenagers are shallow. They want to do something different with their lives.

Ghost World was released in 2001. Probably because of its odd nature, it did not draw a huge audience. However, movie critics loved it. According to the Web site Rotten Tomatoes, 92 percent of critics gave *Ghost World* positive reviews.[10] Critic Joe Baltake of the newspaper the *Sacramento Bee* wrote: "It has qualities—a ferocious wit and a youthful snap and savvy—that can make it irresistible to sophisticated older moviegoers and intelligent teenagers alike."[11] Cathy Thompson-Georges of the Web site BoxOffice.com wrote: "*Ghost World* manages to be grim and hilarious at the same time, not unlike love and adolescence and life itself. Misfits of all stripes (and who doesn't secretly feel like one?) will find that this film is spot-on."[12]

Scarlett won her first acting awards for her performance in *Ghost World*. The organizations that honored her are not common names. However, they are respected in the movie industry. The Chlotrudis Society for Independent Film, a group that celebrates independent and foreign films, gave Scarlett the Chlotrudis Award for best supporting actress. The Toronto Film Critics Association, made up of movie reviewers based in Toronto, Canada, also chose her as best supporting actress for the year. Scarlett was nominated but did not win the best supporting actress honor by the Online Film Critics Society. Members of the Online Film Critics Society are movie reviewers who publish only on the Internet.

Ghost World earned a huge cult following. A cult following is a group of diehard fans who admire a movie so much that they see the movie time and time again. They might go so far as to memorize much of the script and devote fan Web sites to the movie.

Even though Scarlett had a full-time movie career, she was still a high-school student. Aside from juggling her studies around her movie schedule, she also

Scarlett Johansson and Thora Birch play quirky friends Rebecca and Enid in a scene from the film *Ghost World* (2001).

had a social life. When her work on *Ghost World* was finished for the day, she and Thora Birch had fun at the Universal Studios theme park near Los Angeles. They browsed the shops at City Walk and enjoyed some rides. Scarlett wanted to try drag racing, but since Birch did not want to take part, Scarlett drag raced with her brother.

Her first boyfriend was a classical violinist who attended her school. After they split up, she began dating a celebrity—curly-haired singer and musician Jack Antonoff from the band Steel Train. When they were out in public, photographers known as paparazzi, who specialize in celebrity photographs, took candid photos of her. The paparazzi sell the photos to gossip magazines. Scarlett has always been annoyed by that practice. A magazine once asked her to finish the statement, "I sometimes wish I weren't famous, because then I could . . ." Scarlett answered, "not be photographed in private."[13]

But she could not deny the fact that now she was famous.

5
FOUND IN TRANSLATION

Nobody could accuse Scarlett Johansson of being typecast. Consider her next two movie roles.

The first, released in 2001, was titled *An American Rhapsody*. It is a drama set against the backdrop of the Cold War. After World War II ended, the Communist-governed Soviet Union maintained control of nations they were occupying. All these nations were in Eastern Europe and the Soviet Union ran them as dictatorships. One of these nations was Hungary.

Americans were fearful that the Soviet Union was going to try to force Communism on others, including people in the United States. Leaders of the United States and the Soviet Union exchanged angry words and threats. Since no actual fighting between the two nations took place, they were not at war. Instead, the strained relationship between the two superpowers was referred to as the cold war.

An American Rhapsody was based on the life of a Hungarian woman named Éva Gárdos. Gárdos also wrote and directed the movie. In 1950, during the early years of the cold war, Gárdos's parents and older sister bravely escaped Soviet-dominated Hungary. But the parents were forced to leave their infant daughter, Zsuszi, behind. She was raised by a foster family. In 1956, a humanitarian group called the Red Cross brought Zsuszi to the United States. Zsuszi is reunited with her parents and older sister. She also becomes known by the more American name Suzanne. As the movie proceeds, Suzanne grows up. The fifteen-year-old Suzanne is played by Scarlett.

Suzanne is perplexed and troubled. She is living with parents she never knew in a country with different customs than her homeland. She is not sure whether she is Hungarian or an American, or a little of each. At one point, she demands to be sent back to Hungary to learn more about her past.

Rather than film the movie on a studio back lot designed to look like Hungary, Gárdos and the film crew went to Hungary. That was expensive, but it gave the movie a more authentic look. The time away from her boyfriend and much of her family made Scarlett homesick. She might have been a professional actor, but she was still just a fifteen-year-old girl. Those feelings of homesickness did help her get into the character of Suzanne.

Scarlett said, "I was feeling lonely when I was there, even though my mother was with me. We were both kind of feeling a little sad. And that feeling absolutely helped, that nostalgic feeling Suzanne has when she goes back to Hungary."[1] Reviews from professional critics were mixed. Misha Berson of the *Seattle Times* wrote that *An American Rhapsody* is "small in scope but touching and compassionate in its simplicity."[2] Anne Crump of the *San Francisco Examiner* said it is "a film worth seeing if only to watch Scarlett Johansson."[3] But Frank Lovece of *TV Guide's Movie Guide* claimed that Scarlett's depiction of Suzanne made the Hungarian girl seem like "a bratty 15-year-old."[4]

An American Rhapsody was not seen by many. At its peak, it appeared in just fifty-four theaters.[5] It earned a little more than $850 thousand dollars.[6] Major releases that become hits earn tens of millions of dollars. Scarlett tried something new for her next movie. After making several deep movies that made audiences think, she completely shifted gears. She acted in *Eight Legged Freaks*, a horror film about spiders that mutate after exposure to toxic waste and grow to gigantic sizes. *Eight Legged Freaks* is not meant to be taken seriously. It is a comic tribute to a series of similar horror movies made in the 1950s.

Director Ellory Elkayem seems to be winking at his audience throughout the movie, letting them know it is okay to laugh at the gross-out scenes.

In *Eight Legged Freaks*, Scarlett plays Ashley, the teenage daughter of the sheriff in an Arizona town where the giant spiders eat humans for snacks. She finds herself in situations where she has to fight the spider monsters. The spiders are computer generated, though, and were added after the filming. So when filming was taking place, Scarlett had to shoot imaginary spiders, pretending to blast them into smithereens. She said, "I kept thinking, 'What would I do if a 6-foot spider were coming at me?'"[7] Luckily, she is not scared of spiders.

Being an actor is not always glamorous. While the spiders were computer generated, there were real special effects that were truly messy. Scarlett related, "I got attacked, sprayed and gooed with corn syrup and disgusting things that tasted terrible. It took hours to wash the goo out."[8]

But why after being part of so many serious films did Scarlett choose to act in a silly movie such as *Eight Legged Freaks?* She answered matter-of-factly, "Working with giant spiders is something I've never done."[9]

Eight Legged Freaks received mixed reviews. Typical were Stephen Hunter's comments in the *Washington Post.* Hunter wrote: "The movie is a lot more interested in amusing you than frightening you. It seems based more on providing the giggly pleasure of the sudden start, when something pops out of nowhere, than on the morbid shock of seeing others of your species stalked and dismembered."[10] Scarlett was seventeen when *Eight Legged Freaks* was released in the summer of 2002. In many ways she was a typical teenager. She said at the time that she liked shopping for clothes, going to concerts, visiting Disney World, and baked potato day at school.[11] Yet unlike most other teens,

Scarlett comes face-to-face with a giant mutated spider in the 2002 film *Eight Legged Freaks*.

she knew what she wanted to do with the rest of her life. She wanted to keep acting in movies and some day direct them. Her personal goals included making a movie with Woody Allen or Tim Burton, two of the industry's best directors. Her immediate plans were to graduate high school and enroll in college at New York University's respected Tisch School of the Arts. However, she was not accepted by the school.

So Scarlett went back to acting. She traded spiders in Arizona for a part as a lonely, young American wife visiting Japan. The movie was called *Lost in Translation*. Like many of her movies, this was another independent character study. What made it stand out at first was the writer, producer, and director—who was one person. Her name is Sofia Coppola. She was famous at the time for being the daughter of noted director Francis Ford Coppola. He is best known for directing the mob movie *The Godfather* and its two sequels. Since Sofia Coppola has so much respect for Scarlett's acting talent, she did not ask Scarlett to audition for *Lost in Translation*. That is very unusual for such a young actor.

Lost in Translation captures the feelings people get when they travel far away on business trips. They often get lonely. They often feel confused, especially in foreign countries where the national language is different from their own. They sometimes feel jet lag. That happens when airplanes travel through many time zones on one flight. Passengers feel tired at a time of day when they should be wide awake, or vice versa.

In *Lost in Translation*, Scarlett plays Charlotte, a young woman married to a photographer on assignment in Tokyo. Her husband is so busy with his job that he neglects Charlotte. She is often left alone in her hotel room or on her own to walk through the city.

Another person staying at the same hotel is Bob Harris, played by veteran actor and comedian Bill Murray. Bob is a middle-aged actor with a sad face. Bob's career is on the downslide. He has not had a successful acting job for a long time. The only reason he is in Tokyo is to shoot a whisky commercial. It is the only work he can get at this point in his life. Bob is married, but his wife is back home in Los Angeles. She talks to him in Tokyo by phone. The audience can tell by their phone conversations that their marriage is empty.

Charlotte and Bob meet in the hotel and form a strange friendship. The one thing that they really have in common is that they are both lonely Americans in a foreign country. The movie follows their friendship. The audience wonders if they will become a romantic couple despite the difference in their ages.

Johansson and Murray did not meet beforehand to get to know each other. Johansson said, "We met and literally started filming the next day. But it wasn't really important to establish anything, because the characters meet in Tokyo just like we did."[12]

Johansson was seventeen when the filming of *Lost in Translation* began. She was eighteen when it finished. Yet she plays a married woman who is supposed to be about twenty-two or twenty-three. That is a reversal of many movies in which young-looking actors in their twenties are cast to play teenagers. Even though she had just graduated high school, Johansson was mature enough to play an older, married woman.

People looking for a lot of action will be disappointed in *Lost in Translation.* There are some funny scenes and some tender ones. But there are no car crashes, explosions, or frantic chases. And Johansson also gets to sing in the movie. She can be heard covering the Pretenders' hit, "Brass in Pocket."

Bill Murray and Scarlett Johansson in 2003's *Lost in Translation*. It was her role in this movie that made her a household name.

Near the end of the movie Bob accidentally meets Charlotte on a street in downtown Tokyo. He whispers something in her ear, but the audience never gets to hear it. That scene is very memorable, and people who saw the movie tried to guess what Bob says to her. When asked what Bob says to Charlotte, Johansson admitted only that she was caught up in the feelings of her character. Johansson conceded, "I'm not going to be obnoxious and say, 'You're a nosy journalist for asking, and it's for you to find out,' although it really is. Bill said a lot of things to me, silly things. But whatever he said filled me with emotion. I was a mess; I didn't expect to get that sad."[13]

Some time later, someone posted a clip online of that emotional scene with phony dialogue dubbed in. When asked about it in 2008, Johansson was dismayed. "I didn't even know about that clip," she said. "Nothing was written for that scene and we did it so many times that I really couldn't tell you what was said. I think it's unfortunate that people can't appreciate the filmmaker's decision to not have that heard. There's poetry in that scene. People are obsessed with discovering the secret of everything and uncovering the code. That's sad."[14]

Like Robert Redford years earlier, director Sofia Coppola found Scarlett Johansson to be poised and mature. Coppola said, "She makes you feel like she has been around the world. She has a coolness and a subtlety that you would not expect. You feel likes she's seen a lot. She can convey an emotion without saying very much at all."[15]

Being away from home for twenty-seven days filming in Tokyo made Johansson lonely and depressed. Thankfully her mother/manager was with her in Tokyo. She felt better by giving her mother a goodnight kiss at the end of each day. Johansson admitted that being in Tokyo was "like being on another planet."[16] She said, "I was like, 'Mom, you have to stay with me. I cannot be left here alone.' I am young. I need a little TLC."[17]

The response to *Lost in Translation* was overwhelming. An astounding total of 94 percent of the critics on the Rotten Tomatoes Web site gave it positive reviews.[18] According to David Ansen of *Newsweek:* "In Coppola's *Lost in Translation,* Johansson finally takes center stage and becomes an adult."[19] Eleanor Ringel Gillespie, movie critic for the *Atlanta Journal-Constitution,* noted: "This is Johansson's breakthrough role."[20]

Critic James Berardinelli of the Reelviews Web site fully agreed. He said her performance in *Lost in Translation* is her best to date.[21] Berardinelli added, "Her performance is so real and so unfazed and so natural and you believed so much in that character. I think that's the difference between a good performance and a great performance. I would rank that as one of the best movies of the last decade."[22]

Numerous critics and journalists thought Johansson would be nominated for an Academy Award for her acting in *Lost in Translation.* Surprisingly that did not happen. James Berardinelli believes that had to do more with the movie business than her acting skills.

Berardinelli explained that major movie studios spend much time and money promoting their movies so people will vote for them during Academy Awards balloting. He added that the producers of *Lost in Translation* did not have a huge budget to do that kind of promoting.

Berardinelli noted: "A lot of money is put into advertising [by the studios]. They have banquets and galas and they trot their stars out to do all they can to promote their movie. The Oscars are fifty percent what's on the screen and fifty percent what's behind the scenes."[23]

However, within the next year she did receive a hearty share of other nominations. At least a half dozen different city critics' associations nominated her for best actress. She won one of those awards, from the Boston Society of Film Critics.

Johansson was nominated for a respected Golden Globe award. The category was best actress in a motion picture musical or comedy. Golden Globes are given by the Hollywood Foreign Press Association (HFPA), which consists of movie critics from outside the United States who cover American-made movies.

However, the award went to veteran actor Diane Keaton for a little-seen movie, *Something's Gotta Give*. But Johansson did win a different important film award—a BAFTA. BAFTAs are given by the British Academy of Film and Television Arts. They are commonly referred to as the British Oscars.

Upon receiving her honor at the awards ceremony, she said to the crowd, "This is really unexpected. I want to thank my mother Melanie for supporting me and being there for me, taking me to auditions and buying me a hotdog afterwards."[24]

The *London Telegraph* later named *Lost in Translation* one of the movies that defined the decade. The *Telegraph* wrote about the movie: "Dreamy not-quite romance, about a young American girl wandering through Tokyo with a faded actor, made Scarlett Johansson a star."[25]

6

THE QUEEN OF INDEPENDENTS

*T*he *Horse Whisperer* might have made Scarlett Johansson a respected actor. But *Lost in Translation* made her world famous. Suddenly, everybody wanted to learn more about her.

What people learned is that she is hardly a typical star. For one thing, she successfully grew from child actor to adult actor. Critic James Berardinelli stressed that that is not an easy feat. He said, "She survived that transition from child actor to adult actor. That transition didn't kill her like it has killed many child actors."[1]

In addition, Johansson does not live what many see as a usual celebrity lifestyle. She does not spend all night at parties trying to get her picture in the newspapers, magazines, or on online gossip sites. Some entertainers and their managers believe the show-business saying, "Any publicity is good publicity." That means that even if an actor makes news for something bad, at least his or her name is in the public eye. That way people will not forget about the actor.

Johansson is a very private person. She confessed, "I can't stand those articles where people spill their life story. After a while I feel like I know more about them than their best friend does—and that's weird. It's better when you don't know everything."[2]

Like most teenagers, she liked to go to parties. However, she attended these gatherings merely to enjoy herself and be with her friends, not to be seen— something that is not easy for a successful actor. In one interview, she said she prefers to hang around in her New York City apartment. One of her favorite activities is to stretch out on the sofa with a good book and her Chihuahua, Maggie. Rather than eating at a gourmet restaurant with other celebrities, she is just as happy chowing down on Chinese food delivered to her apartment.

On a typical day, Johansson says, "I walk my dog. I fill my gas tank. I go to cafes and have sandwiches."[3] A favorite meal is a slice of vegetarian pizza and a Diet Coke. She may have a piece of key lime pie for dessert. For fun, she might walk around New York and pay a visit to the Central Park Zoo. She likes shopping, but not always at ritzy stores such as Saks Fifth Avenue. Johansson favors finding funky and cheap clothing at thrift and vintage shops in the Greenwich Village and Lower East Side neighborhoods of the city.

Johansson admitted, "I'm pretty casual. I wear vintage sneakers and flats. I can walk in heels, but do I wear them every day? Certainly not. Only if I'm going to a premiere or party, because I like to look like a lady."[4]

But because she is famous, Johansson is often the subject of articles she has nothing to do with. Tabloids, or gossip magazines, make a lot of money publishing articles about the personal lives of celebrities. Johansson detests them and says they are usually not true. She says, "I read about myself dating people I've never met."[5] When asked if she has a boyfriend, Scarlett answers, "I don't want to talk about my personal life. I never said I was dating anybody, but people make things up and start following you around anyway."[6]

Johansson also gives a thumbs-down to drug use. "I've had the problem of dating a cocaine addict. It was horrible. I won't allow myself to get involved with somebody like that again because you are never as important as the drug."[7] She added, "I have a really wonderful family that's very supportive. Luckily I never really struggled with any kind of image problems or addictions."[8] She stresses that drugs and other problems are not limited to actors and other people in the public eye. It is a temptation many young people face. "It's not just people in Hollywood. . . . It's kind of part of just growing up and growing up in the world that we live in today where everything is so available and so fast-paced."[9]

Johansson is different from many other female actors in another way. She is not tall or stick thin. In a time when female actors seem to believe the expression, "You can never be too rich or too thin," Johansson disagrees—especially about the "too thin" part. She stands either five foot three inches, or five foot four inches, depending on the source. She is known for having a figure like Marilyn Monroe.

Johansson says, "I'm curvy—I'm never going to be 5'11" and 120 pounds. But I feel lucky to have what I've got."[10] She thinks being ultrathin is not only unattractive but unhealthy as well.[11] Referring to fashion models, she says, "You go to a runway show, and the model is a hanger for the dress. Nobody has that body! It's disturbing."[12]

Speaking to young people, she said, ""I try to stay fit and eat healthily, but I'm not anxious to starve myself and become unnaturally thin. I don't find that look attractive on women and I don't want to become part of that trend. It's unhealthy and it puts too much pressure on women in general who are being fed this image of the ideal, which it is not. I think America has become obsessed with dieting rather than focusing on eating well, exercising and living a healthy life. . . . Women shouldn't be forced to conform to unrealistic and unhealthy body images that the media promote."[13]

Johansson added she thinks being confident, not unusually thin, is the key to being attractive.[14]

Meanwhile, Johansson's star continued to rise. She took a lead role in another movie not made by a big Hollywood studio. It is titled *Girl With a Pearl Earring*. That is also the name of a famous painting by Dutch artist Johannes Vermeer, who lived in the 1600s. Not much is known about the girl in Vermeer's painting. Some believe the girl was Vermeer's sixteen-year-old maid. In the movie, Johansson plays Vermeer's maid, who is named Griet.

The movie tries to tell the story of the painting. The story line implies that Vermeer and Griet were in love, even though Vermeer is married. The characters are similar in some ways to those of *Lost in Translation*. Like Bill Murray's character, Bob Harris, Vermeer has an unhappy marriage. Also like Bob Harris, Vermeer finds a companion in a much younger girl who inspires him.

Since so little is known about Vermeer, the plot is mostly guesswork. That does not make the story any less intriguing. Johansson spends most of the movie with her beautiful hair pinned up under a white bonnet in the style of the mid-1600s. She also has very few lines. Johansson shows what Griet is thinking mostly through her facial expressions. Critic Richard Roeper said, "For the first time in her brilliant young career, Scarlett Johansson is the centerpiece of a film—and she carries it mostly through her wonderfully expressive face."[15]

Girl With a Pearl Earring was the product of a first-time director, Peter Webber. While making the movie, Webber soon realized that working with Johansson also meant working closely with her mother and manager, Melanie Sloan. Webber said, "Her mother was incredibly helpful to us. She understood the kind of film we were trying to make. She can be tough if things aren't happening the way she needs them to be, but she has to be tough because it's her daughter."[16] Webber respects Sloan enough to give her a "special thanks" in the movie's credits.

As with her previous hit, *Lost in Translation*,

Johansson plays a seventeenth-century maid, the muse of Dutch painter Johannes Vermeer, in *Girl With a Pearl Earring*. This is a recreation of the famous painting with Scarlett Johansson as Griet.

Johansson was nominated for several acting honors. Again, she was ignored by the Oscars. Most of her nominations came from British film groups. She was again nominated for a BAFTA, for best actress in a leading role. She lost—to herself—for her performance in *Lost in Translation.* She was also nominated for a Golden Globe for best actress. Unlike the BAFTAs, she did not compete against herself. Golden Globes categories are more specific than those of the BAFTAs and Oscars. While *Lost in Translation* was put in the category of motion picture comedy or musical, *Girl With a Pearl Earring* was placed in the category of motion picture drama. She lost to Charlize Theron, who played a murderer in the movie *Monster.*

Girl With a Pearl Earring was given positive reviews by the majority of critics.[17] Even though it did not play in many theaters, the movie made over $31 million dollars.[18] (The cost to make the movie is not public information.)

Johansson did not have as much luck with her next movie, *The Perfect Score.* It was released in January 2004 and was her first bomb since she was a child. The plot is about six high-school seniors who decide to break into the Princeton Testing Center in New Jersey that develops the Scholastic Aptitude Tests (SATs). The seniors want to steal the answers to their upcoming SATs so they all can get perfect scores. High-school seniors applying for college must take these tests and send their scores to the colleges they apply to. Johansson plays Francesca Curtis, a girl from a wealthy family.

Very few critics liked *The Perfect Score*. At some point in the movie, each of the six students gives a monologue about his or her goals, hopes, and dreams. Critic Mick LaSalle of the *San Francisco Examiner* thought that the script was poorly written. He wrote: "These monologues are the best thing about 'The Perfect Score,' because they're funny, though they're not intended to be."[19] Other movie reviewers said the direction was poor and the characters were not sympathetic. However, several reported that Johansson's performance was the only good thing about *The Perfect Score*. Typical was Scott Weinberg of the Web site eFilmCritic. According to Weinberg, "Were it not for the recent 'Hollywood Arrival' of one Scarlett Johansson (thanks to her work in *Lost in Translation* and *Girl With a Pearl Earring*), *The Perfect Score* would probably still be holding down that dusty old shelf in the Paramount Pictures - Do Not Release office. Aside from Scarlett, there's not one acting performance in evidence that ranks above *plain old bad*."[20]

The year 2004 was a presidential election year. Democrat John Kerry, a senator from Massachusetts, was running for president against sitting president George W. Bush. Johansson actively campaigned for Kerry. However, Bush won a close but decisive victory in the November election. Johansson publicly said, "[I was] disappointed. I think it was a disappointment for a large percentage of the population."[21] In taking a public stand, she made some enemies among Republican moviegoers. People who disagreed with her views posted nasty comments about her on Web sites.

Even though she is famous and has to deal with all sorts of opinions from critics, she gets hurt by such mean-spirited comments on Web sites. It does not matter if they are about her politics or other personal subjects. Because she is not tall and willowy, some online posters call her fat. She relates, "I went online and found this thing: 'Oh God, she's so ugly and she's so not talented.' I don't understand what the big deal is . . . I was, like: 'Why are you being so mean? I'd like to know what you look like.' And who has the time to go online and talk about people they've never met."[22]

Johansson was able to forget her disappointment when she celebrated her twentieth birthday later in November. She partied with friends at one of her favorite places: Disneyland.

Internet users who did not like her looks were clearly in the minority. Cosmetic companies and fashion designers are always looking for attractive people to help sell their products. In 2004, Scarlett Johansson was hired to model in ads for products made by famous designers Louis Vuitton, Estée Lauder, and Calvin Klein.

Johansson was elated by the news. She said, "Just when I thought things couldn't get better, something like this happens. Being associated with Calvin Klein is a real thrill."[23] The thrill also made Johansson a rich young woman. Calvin Klein paid her $1 million a year for two years.[24]

At the end of 2004, anyone who wanted to see or hear Scarlett Johansson on screen did not have to look very far. As if to prove that she can handle a wide range of roles, Johansson played a part in a movie in which she did not appear on screen. After taking adult roles in *Lost in Translation* and *The Girl With the Pearl Earring*, Johansson did a part in the cartoon film *The SpongeBob SquarePants Movie*. She did the voice of Mindy, King Neptune's daughter.

Doing the voice-over for a cartoon character might seem a strange choice for a serious actor. However, this was a time when several hit animated movies had been released. These included *Shrek*, *Shark Tale*, and *Antz*. In addition, the Nickelodeon television program, *SpongeBob SquarePants* had a following of adult fans who liked its quirky characters and odd story lines.

Johansson joked that one reason she took the role was because she had had a crush on actor David Hasselhoff, who also did a character voice. She admitted, "I so fancied him when I was young that to see my name on the credits next to his makes me go all girly. He was a hunk back in those days."[25] Another reason may have been her business sense. The cartoon movie made a ton of money. It cost only $30 million to make but earned back over $140 worldwide.[26]

During the last week of December 2004, three movies featuring Johansson were released. All were independent films. One titled *In Good Company* is a satire about business. In the movie, a twenty-six-year-old man played by Topher Grace becomes the boss of a fifty-one-year-old veteran, played by Dennis Quaid, in advertising sales. That is awkward in itself. Then the young boss starts dating the older man's daughter, played by Johansson. *In Good Company* did not get nominated for any major awards, but the majority of its reviews were good. David Ansen of *Newsweek* wrote that "Johansson adds spice to the movie's considerable charm."[27] The movie made $61 million in theaters around the world.[28]

Another late 2004 film featuring Scarlett Johansson was *A Good Woman*. This movie is the third retelling based on a play written by Irish playwright Oscar Wilde in 1892. *A Good Woman* had a limited release, so not too many people saw it. And most critics said it did not live up to the wit of Wilde's original play. Some said that the actors were miscast. Even Johansson's performance received poor reviews. *USA Today's* Claudia Puig said that Johansson's portrayal of Lady Windemere was "flat' and "closer to mediocre."[29]

The third movie featuring Johansson that hit the

theaters in late December was *A Love Song for Bobby Long*. Like *A Good Woman*, it also had a limited release in theaters. The movie is a character study about a girl named Pursy Will, played by Johansson. Pursy learns that her mother died in her hometown of New Orleans. She inherits her mother's house. That means she is legally given ownership of the house upon her mother's death.

Pursy returns to the house, expecting to find it empty. Instead, two of her mother's male friends who have become alcoholics are living inside it. Since Pursy is the legal owner of the house, she moves in. But she does not kick the two men out. After living with them for some time, she learns more and more about her mother's life.

A Love Song for Bobby Long received a wide range of reviews. Some critics loved it while others thought it was filled with clichés. Some compared it negatively to the works of legendary playwright Tennessee Williams, who wrote about similar themes. Others said Johansson seemed too worldly to play such a role. Still, enough reviewers liked her performance since she was nominated for, but did not win, a Golden Globe award for best actress in a motion picture drama.

Even though the movie was about people in the American South, it made much more money overseas than in the United States. In the United States it earned just over $164 thousand dollars. Yet it earned over ten times as much—over $1.6 million—in theaters in foreign countries.[30]

Johansson took another departure from character study movies in her next featured role. She costarred in 2005 in a loud and explosive filled sci-fi action thriller titled *The Island.* It played to mixed reviews and made a small profit. But in Johansson's near future was a working relationship with a distinguished director that would redefine Scarlett Johansson's reputation as an actor.

7

WOODY'S MUSE?

After making so many movies in such a short period, Johansson planned to spend some time relaxing. Then she received a message from director and screenwriter Woody Allen. He was planning to shoot his next movie in London. It was a combination crime drama and romance titled *Match Point*. Years ago, Johansson had said she dreamed of working for Allen. Now Allen wanted to know if she wanted to be the lead female in his next movie.

For four decades, Woody Allen has made award-winning movies. They had always been more popular with critics than with audiences. Most were fairly short—about an hour and a half long—and were set in Allen's hometown, New York City. Unlike some male filmmakers, Allen has long been admired for writing realistic and complex roles for women. Several female actors in Allen's movies went on to win Academy Awards. These include Diane Wiest, Diane Keaton, Mira Sorvino, and Penelope Cruz.

Allen's original choice to play the female lead was British actress Kate Winslet. However, Winslet said that she wanted some time off to spend with her family.[1]

Johansson jumped at the chance to work with Allen. She exclaimed, "Woody? Oh, my God, I can't believe it!"[2]

Although Allen is old enough to be Johansson's grandfather, the two clicked right away. She said, "I just adore Woody. We have a lot in common. We're New Yorkers, Jewish. We have a very easy-going relationship."[3]

Allen praised Johansson in return. He raved, "Scarlett is just a naturally great actress. She can do no wrong and is incapable of a bad moment. . . . She was just touched by God."[4]

Most critics loved *Match Point*. Many echoed Mick Martin and Marsha Porter, who wrote that *Match Point* was "Woody Allen's best work in years."[5] Movie reviewer Bill Muller of the *Arizona Republic* wrote, "It's a film worth seeing several times. If you're lucky enough to get the chance."[6]

Johansson plays Nola Rice, a budding American actress engaged to a British man. But complications arise when her fiancé's brother-in-law, a professional tennis player, becomes attracted to her. In time, a murder takes place. There are several themes to *Match Point*, but above all, Johansson explained, "It's really a story about luck, destiny and fate—about what they all mean and if there even are such things."[7]

Again, Johansson's performance received high marks. Paul Clinton of CNN.com wrote: "As for Johansson, she's as alluring and beautiful as always. But she has more: It's amazing that an actress this young has such a strong, sophisticated presence on the screen. Her character also walks a tightrope between

Director Woody Allen talks to Johansson on the set of his 2005 movie *Match Point*.

being sympathetic and contemptible and Johansson steers Nola through these dark waters with great skill."[8]

She was again nominated for acting awards. One came from the Chicago Film Critics Association. The category was best supporting actress. She was also nominated for a Golden Globe for best supporting actress in a motion picture. Unfortunately she did not win either.

While many of Allen's movies have been hits with critics, they often do not draw big numbers of theatergoers. *Match Point* was an exception. It cost $15 million to make but earned over $85 million in both the United States and foreign countries.[9] Typical for Allen's movies, *Match Point* pulled in nearly three times as much money in overseas theaters than in the United States.[10]

The two got along so well that Allen asked Johansson to appear in his next movie, *Scoop*. This movie also takes place in London. This time Johansson plays a bookish American journalism student named Sondra Pransky. Pransky stumbles upon the trail of a serial killer and tries to identify him. Despite the serious subject matter, *Scoop* is part mystery, comedy, and romance.

In his earlier years, Allen used some of the same female actors in many movies. Two of his favorites were Diane Keaton and Mia Farrow. For a while, Allen had a romantic relationship with Farrow. Since these women seemed to inspire Allen, members of the press referred to them as Allen's muses. In Greek mythology, muses are goddesses who inspire creators of literature and art.

Now reporters were giving that title to Johansson. Writer Brian D. Johnson of *Maclean's* magazine wrote that Johansson "appears to be his new muse."[11] Johansson gushed to Johnson, "Woody was more than I ever could have asked for. If he asks me to do anything ever, I would work with him in a heartbeat."[12]

However, Johansson laughed at the idea of being Allen's muse. She said, "I've seen things like, 'Are you his new muse?' Yeah, I go over at 2 A.M. and make him grilled cheese sandwiches, and he writes. Ha. It's just a very easy friendship."[13]

So was she Woody Allen's muse or wasn't she? It depends whether one thinks Johansson was joking or being serious.

Regardless, Allen took a fatherly interest in her. He said, "She's so gifted, she's funny, she can sing, she can act dramatically, she can do anything, but she's gotta make the right choices of films and she's got to not go the Page Six party route." (Page six in the *New York Post*, a daily tabloid newspaper, is devoted to gossip). "I don't want to read about her in the paper with this boyfriend or that boyfriend, or in rehab or taking pills. Now I haven't—which is great—but she's got to keep her poise and select good pictures."[14]

Scoop was released July 28, 2006. It earned only $39 million across the world.[15] The reviews were mixed but mostly negative. The general feeling was that it was a weak rehash of Allen's earlier movies. Some critics said that Johansson was not the right actor to play a mousy student.

Then again, Johansson also received her fair share of praise. Movie reviewer Alex Sandell of the Web site The Juicy Cerebellum wrote: "I worried that Scarlett Johansson wouldn't have the comic chops for a film like this, but she delivers. Her performance is an absolute delight to watch. I knew the actress had talent, but I didn't know she had *timing*. It's hard to make comedy look easy, but Johansson somehow manages."[16]

Sandell also compared Johansson to one of Allen's former favorite actresses. He said, "Johansson brings out the funny in Allen like nobody since Diane Keaton."[17]

In 2006, Johansson signed a lucrative contract, but it had nothing to do with starring in more movies. The internationally known cosmetic company, L'Oreal, offered her the opportunity to be its spokesmodel. Johansson's job was to represent L'Oreal in advertisements for the next four years. It has also been estimated that L'Oreal paid her $3 million a year for this work.[18] Again, Scarlett Johansson proved that a woman does not have to be tall and painfully thin to represent beauty.

Johansson admitted, "I'm never going to look at a picture of Uma Thurman and think I can have her body. It's not what I'm supposed to look like. I once heard that women dress for women—not for men—and I think that has some truth to it. Men, what do they know? They don't know if you gain or lose five pounds. They're oblivious to those kinds of things. A lot of men will say, 'I like you as you are.' And you're like, 'But I'm bloated!' If they're attracted to you, they're attracted to you."[19]

Being a private person, Johansson refuses to discuss her romantic life with reporters. Sometimes gossip reporters and paparazzi would see her in a public place with a single man. So they reported that she was dating that person. Much of the time, Johansson and her companion were just coworkers or friends.

However, it was known about this time that she was dating actor and musician Jared Leto, who was thirteen years older than Johansson. But the two stopped dating before she began work on her next film, *The Black Dahlia*. In *The Black Dahlia*, Johansson stars opposite a handsome actor named Josh Hartnett. At the time, Hartnett was twenty-eight years old. Before long, the two were dating. While Johansson and Leto dated mainly for fun, Johansson and Hartnett were a more serious couple. Scarlett Johansson said of her new boyfriend, "He's just lovely. He's very sensitive and a great guy all around."[20]

The Black Dahlia is a crime story based loosely on a real-life grisly murder. A young woman named Elizabeth "Betty" Short was murdered in Los Angeles in January 1946. Short had hoped to be an actress. "The Black Dahlia" was a nickname reporters had given her. Johansson plays a woman dating two police detectives.

Unfortunately, the best thing about the movie for Johansson may have been meeting Hartnett. *The Black Dahlia* did nothing for her career. Most critics felt the plot was too contrived and the acting was weak. Even Johansson, who often received good reviews in poorly received movies, was panned for her work. Several critics thought she was not convincing playing a character from the 1940s. But others blamed the movie's director, Brian de Palma, for doing a poor job directing the actors.

Unlike some movies that get poor reviews but draw big audiences, *The Black Dahlia* failed on that account, too. It cost $50 million to make and earned back barely over $49 million.[21]

Johansson appeared in one other 2006 movie. It was titled *The Prestige* and was released in October. *The Prestige* is a murder mystery about the rivalry between two young magicians. The setting is England in the late 1890s. When one magician's wife dies, the other magician becomes a suspect. Johansson plays a glamorous magician's assistant. Though it was a sup-porting role, it plays an intricate part in the plot.

Since the movie takes place in England, Johansson had to perfect a convincing British accent. One costar is musician David Bowie, one of Johansson's real-life idols. Bowie plays a surprising role: Nikola Tesla, a scientist and electrical pioneer who discovered the principles of alternating current in 1881.

While *The Prestige* was not nominated for any major awards, it was definitely a success. It received mostly good reviews and also earned back over twice as much as it cost to make.[22]

Josh Hartnett and Johansson in the 2006 crime drama *The Black Dahlia*.

In *The Prestige*, singer David Bowie proved that he could also act. Johansson is an actress who had always wanted to prove she could sing. She almost got the chance in 2006. Award-winning composer Andrew Lloyd Webber was planning to produce a live stage revival in London of the beloved musical, *The Sound of Music*. *The Sound of Music* is based on a true story of a heroic family of Austrian singers around the time the Nazis were taking over Europe. This was just before the start of World War II.

Webber has written such famous musicals as *Cats* and *The Phantom of the Opera*. *The Sound of Music* had been written about fifty years earlier by Broadway legends Richard Rodgers and Oscar Hammerstein II. It was first presented as a Broadway play. Then, in 1965, it was released as a movie. It went on to win the Academy Award for the year's best motion picture. Webber admitted he always loved the show and wanted to produce his own version of it.[23]

He approached Johansson about playing the lead role, Maria von Trapp. She and Webber met in a restaurant to discuss business details. She told Webber that von Trapp was her "dream role."[24] To prove her point, she started singing out loud in the crowded restaurant.

Johansson was all set to sign a contract to play Maria, but it never happened. Some say Johansson's staff wanted more money than Webber offered.

Webber said that Johansson's staff was unaware that live stage does not pay as much as Hollywood movies. Johansson's staff said they simply wanted a fair amount of money for a star as big as Johansson. A different given reason was that the stage play schedule would interfere with Johansson's upcoming movie schedule.[25]

In a bizarre twist, the role of Maria went to a previously unknown singer/actor named Connie Fisher. She won the part in a reality television talent contest similar to *American Idol*. It was broadcast on British television and was titled *How Do You Solve a Problem Like Maria?* That is the title of one of the famous songs from *The Sound of Music*.

Johansson went back to making movies. But she did not give up on her chance to sing.

8

ACTOR AND ALTRUIST

In 2006, Scarlett Johansson was just twenty-one years old, an age when most people are working entry-level jobs or studying in college. Yet she was one of the most recognized faces in the world. But she did not let the fame go to her head. She said, "Someone asked me the other day how it feels to be the hottest young actress in Hollywood. I said it didn't mean anything. Those who are hot eventually cool off. There are a lot of celebrities today who are in a passing phase. Whoever happens to look good in a bikini is the new actress of the moment.

"I'm very serious about my business. I'm also one of four kids, so I was taught at a very early age that my problems weren't the most important in the whole world. That kind of helps to keep your head together. When you come from a big family and not all the attention is focused on you all the time, you learn to balance out what is important and what isn't."[1]

Early in 2007, Johansson's name was in magazines and Web sites for something she would have not preferred. Despite the fact that she likes to keep her personal life private, word got out that she and Josh Hartnett had broken up.

Hartnett said their breakup had to do with the amount of travel involved in their line of work. They spent too much time apart from each other. He admitted the split was "really painful."[2] Hartnett added, "It was difficult spending so much time apart with all our different commitments and both of us flying all over the world. At the end of the day we're just ordinary people and it didn't work."[3]

As usual, Johansson refused to talk about her personal life. However, entertainment journalists said that she was more troubled by her break with Hartnett than with her earlier boyfriends.[4]

By now, Johansson was making more money in a few months than most people make in a lifetime. Even though she was busy with her work schedule, she wanted to give something back to the world. She became active in an organization called Oxfam International. Oxfam is a group of fourteen organizations that fights poverty and oppression worldwide.

It also sends aid to places that have been hit by natural disasters.

Some entertainers have been accused of not being serious about their efforts to help others. Some critics claim they do such good deeds simply for the publicity. That was certainly not true about Johansson. Oxfam itself wrote: "Scarlett Johansson is a passionate and committed advocate and fundraiser."[5]

In the spring of 2007, she skipped the glamour of the Academy Awards ceremony in Los Angeles to travel with Oxfam to India and the neighboring island nation of Sri Lanka. At one point, she stayed in a poverty-stricken part of India called Uttar Pradish. She visited a school that Oxfam had helped build.

Johansson learned that the children of Uttar Pradish sleep on dirt floors in one-room houses. They have no electricity or running water. Some have to skip school during harvest season, when they help their families pick crops. They do not receive money for their work; all they get is a little bit of food. Johansson said, "These kids are working for potatoes. Literally."[6]

The children Johansson visited had no idea that she is famous. They have no access to movie theaters or television sets. They did not see her as anybody special—just a volunteer from Oxfam. Shortly before her trip, Johansson posed as Cinderella in a photo shoot to advertise Disney theme parks. She was paid hundreds of thousands of dollars for the photo shoot. But she gave it all to the community of Uttar Pradish.[7] The money went to support four schools.[8]

Johansson does not stop at helping others by traveling only to foreign countries. One American charity Johansson works with is called USA Harvest. One of USA Harvest's programs is called Blessings in a Backpack. This program makes sure children who get help paying for lunches at school also eat healthily on weekends. Johansson remembers her childhood when she and her siblings ate school lunches that were paid for by the government. She is thrilled to help others now that she has the chance.[9]

She said, "I think, especially now, a lot of people are struggling financially, and a lot of kids don't know where their next meal is coming from. They see their parents trying to scrape together money or welfare or food stamps for meals. For parents to have some relief and know their kids are fed for those extra two days of the week makes a huge difference."[10]

One evening, Johansson was a guest on Jay Leno's TV show when she sneezed into a tissue. Leno joked that people would pay a lot of money for that tissue. Johansson took his joke seriously and agreed to sell it on the auction Web site eBay as long as the money went to USA Harvest. Leno agreed, and the tissue sold for $5,300.[11]

When she was not appearing on television talk shows or volunteering her time and money, Johansson continued to act. She played the lead in *The Nanny Diaries*, which came out in the summer of 2007. The movie is a comedy-drama based on a nonfiction book. Johansson plays Annie Braddock, a college graduate who cannot find a job in her field. She then takes a job as a nanny for a rich, uncaring New York family with a spoiled child.

Most reviews were vicious. The critics' main gripe was that the characters are all clichés. To them, the movie portrays all wealthy people as caring more about social events than the well-being of their children. The critics were mixed in their judgment of Johansson's performance. Many were like John Wirt, film critic for the *Baton Rouge Advocate*. He wrote: "Every character in *The Nanny Diaries* is ill-defined, including Johansson's floundering nanny. Exhibiting a dull to puzzled expression, Johansson gives a shapeless performance in an embarrassing misfire of a movie that goes every which way but right."[12]

However, others panned the movie in general but were pleased with Johansson's performance. One was Sean O'Connell of Filmcritic.com. He wrote that Johansson "showcases her rarely exercised knack for self-deprecating physical comedy as Annie Braddock."[13]

Off the screen, Johansson made news again. In 2007, she began dating another actor, thirty-year-old Ryan Reynolds. When a reporter asked Johansson about him, she responded, "I always hate these questions because they make me feel queasy, and I hate feeling like I have to share my personal life with anybody. So I'll take the normal celebrity route and just say I'm going to keep my personal life private. But I'm very, very happy."[14]

It was also in 2007 that Johansson finally got her chance to sing. Rather than appearing on stage as she would have in *The Sound of Music*, she made a compact disc. It was about as opposite from *The Sound of Music*

Scarlett Johansson and Nicholas Art in *The Nanny Diaries*. The nanny forms a strong bond with the little boy she is hired to look after.

as possible. She recorded a series of songs originally performed by Tom Waits.

Waits is a gravelly-voiced singer and songwriter who has never had huge commercial success. However, he has had a cult following since he first began performing in the early 1970s. He earned a reputation for singing about seedy places in the dark sides of cities.

Johansson is unusual in that she has been a fan of Waits since she was a preteen, when most girls listen to pop singers and boy bands. She explained, "I first got into Tom Waits when I was like, 11, or 12. A friend of mine, her dad listened to Tom Waits all the time, so I was introduced to his music pretty young. Then I had a boyfriend in high school who was a huge Tom Waits fan. I guess Tom Waits was always a part of my adolescence."[15]

She titled the compact disc *Anywhere I Lay My Head*, after a Waits song. It was released May 20, 2008. Reviews were mixed. Music critic Chris Willman of *Entertainment Weekly* said it was the worst CD of 2008.[16] On the other hand, a writer from British magazine *New Musical Express* (*NME*), Priya Elan, countered, "This is a brilliant album that will no doubt top some 'best of 2008 lists.'"[17] Sales of the CD were so-so.

Her next movie, *The Other Boleyn Girl*, is a fictional historical drama that takes place in sixteenth-century England. Mary Boleyn was the sister of Anne Boleyn, the second wife of England's King Henry VIII. The movie depicts both Boleyn girls as rivals for Henry's love. Johansson plays Mary while Natalie Portman plays Anne. The movie had a wide range of reviews, but it earned a profit. That is mainly due to audiences overseas. *The Other Boleyn Girl* cost $35 million to produce and earned back around $27 million in the United States. After it was released overseas, its total earnings reached over $77 million.[18]

Natalie Portman and Johansson play sisters Anne and Mary Boleyn in *The Other Boleyn Girl* (2008).

The reviews were far better for her next movie, *Vicki Cristina Barcelona*. Like *Match Point* and *Scoop*, it was directed by Woody Allen. *Vicki Cristina Barcelona* is set in the romantic city of Barcelona, Spain. It is a romantic comedy-drama about two young American women vacationing in Barcelona. Both become involved with a handsome Spanish painter. Critic Roger Ebert wrote: "The actors are attractive, the city is magnificent, the love scenes don't get all sweaty, and everybody finishes the summer a little wiser and with a lifetime of memories. What more could you ask?"[19]

The film won a Golden Globe Award for best comedy or musical motion picture. However, all the major actors except for Johansson were nominated for Golden Globes—even though none of them won. Penelope Cruz, who played the Spanish artist's high-strung ex-wife, did win the Academy Award for best actress in a supporting role.

If she was disappointed at being ignored by the major awards, Johansson did not publicly say. Meanwhile, she kept busy with her charity work. If auctioning off a used tissue was not wild enough, Johansson took part in another crazy fund-raiser. She auctioned off a twenty-minute-long date with herself on eBay. The winner was a British man who remained anonymous. He won the chance to accompany her to the world premiere of her movie *He's Just Not That Into You* when it was released in 2009. He paid twenty thousand British pounds for the short date. That was equal to more than thirty-two thousand U.S. dollars.[20]

Johansson was thrilled about the money raised. She said, "To get 20,000 pounds for a 20-minute date and a pair of tickets to help us fight poverty is fantastic. All of this money will be used to help us fight poverty in countries all over the world."[21]

She also traveled to the war-ravaged Persian Gulf on behalf of a group called the United Service Organizations (USO). The USO has been providing entertainment and emotional support to American servicemen and servicewomen since the 1940s. Johansson stated, "This USO tour to the Gulf region truly means a lot. I've wanted to go over and visit for some time, and now my moment has arrived. It's one thing to reply to a letter or extend your thanks to

Actor Ryan Reynolds attends the People's Choice Awards in Los Angeles on January 6, 2010. He and Johansson were married on September 27, 2008, in his native Canada.

service members in a speech, but it is another thing to visit them and spend time with those that do so much for us back home."[22]

On September 27, 2008, Johansson and Ryan Reynolds were married. As one might expect, Johansson kept the ceremony very private. The wedding was held not in Los Angeles or New York but in a secluded resort in British Columbia, Canada. Only a small group of family and friends was invited. Gossip columnists and paparazzi tried to crash the ceremony. But Johansson and Reynolds kept tight security. They even kept secret the source where Johansson bought her wedding dress. Said Johansson, "You have to protect some things, even if it is a silly detail like who designed your dress. It was private, which is what I really wanted. I've never been the girl who thought of the big dress, the big ceremony. I'm more low-key than that. Most people want photographers at their wedding, and for us it was how do we keep them out?"[23]

One more movie featuring Johansson was released in 2008, on Christmas Day. Its title is *The Spirit,* and it is a live action crime drama based on a comic-book series. Movie reviewers generally hated *The Spirit.* It received the worst reviews of any of her movies since *North. The Spirit* was not liked by movie audiences either. It played in American theaters for a mere four weeks before it closed.

Movies like *The Spirit* and *The Nanny Diaries*

caused former fans such as James Berardinelli to become more hesitant in their praise. Berardinelli stated: "The last few movies she has been in have not been as good as her early ones. It may be that her directors are not as commanding, or that she is not choosing her roles as well."[24] He wonders if she may put acting on the back burner in a few years and try her luck behind the scenes—such as directing movies rather than acting in them.[25]

The very private actor took one daring step to protect her privacy early in 2009. The British edition of *Cosmopolitan* featured a photograph of Johansson on the cover of its January 2009 issue. Superimposed over her picture was a teaser headline: "Scarlett: Why I had to get married."[26]

Johansson accused *Cosmopolitan* of making up quotes for the article. She and her publicist Marcel Pariseau threatened to sue *Cosmopolitan* unless they admitted the quotes were false.

That was a gutsy move on Johansson's part. Many public figures will let such things slide. By making a public issue of such matters, they sometimes give them more publicity than if they had left them alone. Once the February issue of *Cosmopolitan* was released, the January issue would likely have been tossed away in a recycling bin and forgotten.

But Johansson and Pariseau's move paid off. *Cosmopolitan* publicly apologized to Johansson.

The magazine posted a statement on its Web site: "*Cosmopolitan* would like to apologize to our readers and Scarlett Johansson for inaccuracies in our January issue where we said she talked about her marriage and her relationship with her husband. We now understand Ms. Johansson has not commented publicly on her married life and did not do so on this occasion."[27] The same statement was also published in the magazine's print edition.

Johansson released one movie in 2009, *He's Just Not That Into You*. It was the premiere of this movie that the blind-date auction winner attended with Johansson. *He's Just Not That Into You* is an ensemble movie, meaning that instead of having one lead role surrounded by supporting roles, there are several roles of equal importance. The movie is about the dating life of people in their twenties. It is told mostly from women's point of view, so it is not surprising that most of its audience was women.

And women went to see it in droves. *He's Just Not That Into You* earned over $178 million in both American and foreign theaters.[28] Critics gave it mixed reviews. Some said the characters were not well developed. Others said the story lines were thin. Others felt like critic Mick LaSalle of the *San Francisco Chronicle*. He wrote: "*He's Just Not That Into You* never soars, but it never flags. It remains brisk, engaging and pleasant throughout."[29]

Pete Yorn and Johansson make an appearance at the Bon Marche store in Paris, France, on September 11, 2009, to promote their album *Break Up*.

Johansson was given the opportunity to sing in *He's Just Not That Into you.* She performed a tune called "Last Goodbye." It was originally recorded by folk and alternative rock musician Jeff Buckley.

Johansson then spent more time in the recording studio. She teamed up with rock singer and guitarist Pete Yorn. The two worked together on a compact

Scarlett Johansson and Liev Schreiber onstage opening night of Arthur Miller's play A View From the Bridge on Broadway, January 24, 2010.

disc titled *Break Up*. Most of the songs were written by Yorn. But they were inspired by two albums released in the late 1960s by French actors/singers Serge Gainsbourg and Brigitte Bardot. It was released on September 15, 2009.

Reviews again were mixed, but were better overall than that of her first CD. Leah Greenblatt of *Entertainment Weekly* summed things up by writing: "Johansson's throaty vocals fit *Break Up*'s intimate vibe better than they did on her overly ambitious Tom Waits-covers album."[30] As with *Anywhere I Lay My Head*, sales were adequate but not great.

Johansson and Reynolds ended the decade in a very casual way. The two stars spent New Year's Eve not at a glamorous party. They stayed home, ate some pizza, and watched *The Twilight Zone* marathon on the Syfy network. For one thing, they both had to work on New Year's Day. Also, Johansson said, "Going from one party to the next and surfing to find the right thing, and being in a taxicab when the clock strikes—I'm so over that stuff."[31]

She also spent that winter doing something she had not done since age eight—acting in a professional live New York play. Unlike her minor role in the drama *Sophistry*, Johansson played a major part in the play *A View From the Bridge.* It is a tale of an Italian-American family and was written by famous playwright Arthur Miller. And unlike *Sophistry, A View From the Bridge* was performed on Broadway, not off-Broadway.

A View From the Bridge opened January 24, 2010 and ran for fourteen weeks. In May, Johansson was honored with a Tony award for best featured actress in a play. The Tonys are Broadway's equivalent of the Oscars. Johansson was stunned by the award. As she accepted it, she gushed, "I don't know what to say. Ever since I was a little girl, I wanted to be on Broadway. Here I am. Unbelievable."[32]

She also showed her acting chops in the summer of 2010 by appearing in a movie that was the polar opposite of the serious drama *A View From the Bridge.* It was *Iron Man 2*, based on a comic about a superhero. Johansson played Natasha Romanoff, also known as the "Black Widow," an attractive Russian spy.

The part called for her to fit into a skintight cat suit and do incredible acrobatic scenes. She did a lot to get ready. It included months of stunt and strength training. Johansson was asked what it was like to first step into the cat suit. She answered, "It was crazy to see it for the first time—everything all zipped up and all the weapons in there, bracelets on, the whole look. It was pretty sweet, I have to say."[33]

In December 2010, Johansson and husband Ryan Reynolds were reported to have split from each other. The split was reported to be amicable and had been simply caused by the demands on both actors' time-crunched schedules. Regardless, expect more great things in Johansson's future.

CHRONOLOGY

1984   Scarlett Johansson is born on November 22 in New York City.

1993   Enrolls in Lee Strasberg Theatre Institute for Young People; acts on stage in play *Sophistry*.

1994   First movie, *North,* released; acts in skit on *Late Night With Conan O'Brien* television show.

1995   Movie *Just Cause* is released.

1996   Movies *If Lucy Fell* and *Manny and Lo* released; mother Melanie takes over as manager; nominated for first acting award, Independent Spirit Award, for performance in *Manny and Lo;* starts attending Professional Children's School.

1997   Appears in movies *Fall* and *Home Alone 3.*

1998   Receives national acclaim for her performance in *The Horse Whisperer.*

1999   Appears in movies *My Brother the Pig* and *The Man Who Wasn't There.*

2001   Wins first acting award for her performance in movie *Ghost World;* movie *An American Rhapsody* released.

2002   Appears in movie *Eight Legged Freaks;* graduates from Professional Children's School.

2003   Wins BAFTA award and nominated for Golden Globe for her performance in *Lost in Translation;* nominated for BAFTA and Golden Globe for her performance in *Girl With a Pearl Earring.*

2004   Actively campaigns for Democratic presidential candidate John Kerry; nominated for Golden Globe for movie *A Love Song for Bobby Long*; also appears in movies *The Perfect Score, In Good Company, A Good Woman,* and does voice over in *The SpongeBob SquarePants Movie*; hired to model in ads for designers including Calvin Klein.

2005   First works with Woody Allen; nominated for Golden Globe for her performance in *Match Point*; appears in movie *The Island*.

2006   Featured in movies *Scoop, The Black Dahlia,* and *The Prestige*; hired as spokesmodel for Calvin Klein.

2007   Skips Academy Awards to take humanitarian trip to India and Sri Lanka on behalf of Oxfam; appears in movie *The Nanny Diaries*.

2008   Compact disc *Anywhere I Lay My Head* is released; movies *The Other Boleyn Girl, Vicki Cristina Barcelona,* and *The Spirit* are released; entertains troops in Persian Gulf as part of USO tour; marries Ryan Reynolds on September 27.

2009   Releases second compact disc, *Break Up*; appears in movie *He's Just Not That Into You*.

2010   Acts in Broadway play *A View From the Bridge*; wins Tony award on June 13 for best featured actress in a play; appears in movie *Iron Man 2*.

FILMOGRAPHY

1994	*North*
1995	*Just Cause*
1996	*Manny and Lo* *If Lucy Fell*
1997	*Home Alone 3* *Fall*
1998	*The Horse Whisperer*
1999	*My Brother the Pig* *The Man Who Wasn't There*
2001	*Ghost World* *An American Rhapsody*
2002	*Eight Legged Freaks*
2003	*Lost in Translation* *Girl With a Pearl Earring* *A Love Song for Bobby Long*
2004	*A Good Woman* *The SpongeBob SquarePants Movie* *The Perfect Score* *In Good Company*
2005	*The Island* *Match Point*
2006	*Scoop* *The Black Dahlia* *The Prestige*
2007	*The Nanny Diaries* *The Other Boleyn Girl*
2008	*Vicky Cristina Barcelona* *The Spirit*
2009	*He's Just Not That Into You*
2010	*Iron Man 2*

CHAPTER NOTES

Chapter 1. Not Just Horsing Around

1. Brandon Hurst, *Scarlett Johansson* (London: A Jot Publishing, Ltd., 2009), p. 29.

2. Ibid.

3. Reviews of *The Horse Whisperer,* directed by Robert Redford, *Rotten Tomatoes,* n.d., <http://www.rottentomatoes.com/m/horse_whisperer/> (November 9, 2009).

4. "The Horse Whisperer," *Box Office Mojo,* n.d., <http://boxofficemojo.com/movies/?id=horsewhisperer.htm> (November 9, 2009).

5. James Berardinelli, review of *The Horse Whisperer,* directed by Robert Redford, *Reelviews,* 2010, <http://www.reelviews.net/php_review_template.php?identifier=115> (October 26, 2009).

6. William Keck, "New Year Bright for Johansson," *USA Today,* December 28, 2004, <http://www.usatoday.com/life/people/2004-12-28-johansson-main_x.htm> (October 13, 2009).

Chapter 2. "I Wanted to Be Judy Garland"

1. Rebecca Winters Keegan, "Red-Hot Scarlett," *Cosmopolitan,* August 2008, p. 40.

2. Gina Shaw, "Scarlett Johansson Feeds Hungry Children," *WebMD,* October 28, 2009, <http://children.webmd.com/features/scarlett-johansson-feeds-hungry-children?print=true#> (November 24, 2009).

3. Ibid.

4. Sanjiv Bhattacharya, "Scarlett in Bloom," *New York,* February 16, 2004, <http://nymag.com/nymetro/shopping/fashion/spring04/n_9843/> (November 23, 2009).

5. Anthony Weiss, "The Scarlett Grandma," *Forward,* April 7, 2006, <http://www.forward.com/articles/1188/> (August 23, 2010).

6. James Kaplan, "More Than a Pretty Face," *Parade,* February 27, 2007, <http://www.parade.com/articles/ editions/2007/edition_03-11-2007/Scarlett_Johansson> (October 13, 2009).

7. Melena Ryzik, "Local Favourite," *Sydney Morning Herald,* September 17, 2007, <http://www.smh.com.au/ news/film/local-favourite/2007/09/16/1189881329353.html> (October 13, 2009).

8. Karen S. Schneider, Rebecca Paley, and Alison Singh Gee, "Real Attitude," *People,* October 6, 2003, <http://www. people.com/people/archive/article/0,,20148275,00.html> (August 23, 2010).

9. Polly Vernon, "Scarlett Fever," *London Guardian,* December 28, 2003, <http://www.guardian.co.uk/film/2003/ dec/28/features.magazine> (November 17, 2009).

10. Ibid.

11. Ibid.

12. Ibid.

13. Chris Roberts, *Scarlett Johansson: Portrait of a Rising Star* (London: Carlton Books, 2007), p. 22.

Chapter 3. Playing Manny and Molly

1. Sanjiv Bhattacharya, "Scarlett in Bloom," *New York,* February 16, 2004, <http://nymag.com/nymetro/shopping/ fashion/spring04/n_9843/> (November 23, 2009).

2. Roger Ebert, review of *North,* directed by Rob Reiner, *RogerEbert.com,* July 22, 1994, <http://rogere-bert.suntimes.com/apps/pbcs.dll/article?AID=/19940722/ REVIEWS/407220302/1023> (November 23, 2009).

3. Hal Hinson, review of *Just Cause,* directed by Arne Glimcher, *Washington Post,* February 17, 1995, <http://www. washingtonpost.com/wp-srv/style/longterm/movies/videos/ justcauserhinson_c0098d.htm> (November 24, 2009).

4. Christopher Null, review of *If Lucy Fell,* directed by Eric Schaeffer, *Filmcritic.com,* March 6, 1996, <http://www. filmcritic.com/misc/emporium.nsf/reviews/If-Lucy-Fell> (November 25, 2009).

5. James Berardinelli, review of *If Lucy Fell,* directed by Eric Schaeffer, *Reelviews,* 1996, <http://www.reelviews.net/ movies/i/if_lucy.html> (November 25, 2009).

6. Keith Dovkants, "Scarlett's Journey to the Top," *London Evening Standard,* February 18, 2004, <http://www. thisislondon.co.uk/film/article-9210050-scarletts-journey-to-the-top.do> (November 25, 2009).

7. Barbara Shulgasser, "Many Things to Like About 'Manny & Lo,'" *San Francisco Examiner,* August 9, 1996, <http://www.sfgate.com/cgi-bin/article.cgi?f=/e/a/1996/08/09/ WEEKEND6031.dtl> (November 25, 2009).

8. Ibid.

9. Personal interview with James Berardinelli, January 27, 2010.

10. James Berardinelli, review of *Manny and Lo,* directed by Lisa Krueger, *Reelviews,* 1996, <http://www.reelviews.net/ php_review_template.php?identifier=114> (November 25, 2009).

11. Brandon Hurst, *Scarlett Johansson* (London: A Jot Publishing, Ltd., 2009), p. 27.

12. "Home Alone 3," *Box Office Mojo,* n.d. <http://boxoficemojo.com/movies/?id=homealone3.htm> (November 26, 2009).

Chapter 4. Scarlett the Starlet

1. Polly Vernon, "Scarlett Fever," *London Guardian,* December 28, 2003, <http://www.guardian.co.uk/film/2003/ dec/28/features.magazine> (November 17, 2009).

2. Ibid.

3. Ibid.

4. James Kaplan, "More Than a Pretty Face," *Parade,* February 27, 2007, <http://www.parade.com/articles/ editions/2007/edition_03-11-2007/Scarlett_Johansson> (October 13, 2009).

5. Mick Martin and Marsha Porter, *DVD and Video Guide 2007* (New York: Ballantine Books, 2006), p. 774.

6. Todd McCarthy, review of *The Man Who Wasn't There,* directed by Joel Coen, *Variety,* May 13, 2001, <http://www.variety.com/review/VE1117798042. html?categoryid=31&cs=1> (November 30, 2009).

7. A. J. Jacobs, "Scarlett Johansson Is the Sexiest Woman Alive, 2006," *Esquire,* November 2006, <http://www.esquire. com/women/women-we-love/scarlett-johansson-pics> (August 23, 2010).

8. Ibid.

9. Ibid.

10. Reviews of *Ghost World,* directed by Terry Zwigoff, *Rotten Tomatoes,* n.d., <http://www.rottentomatoes.com/m/ ghost_world/?critic=columns&sortby=name&name_order= asc&view=#contentReviews> (June 24, 2010).

11. Ibid.

12. Cathy Thompson-George, review of *Ghost World,* directed by Terry Zwigoff, *Box Office Magazine,* July 19, 2001, <http://boxoffice.com/reviews/2008/08/ghost-world.php> (November 30, 2009).

13. Rebecca Winters Keegan, "Red-Hot Scarlett," *Cosmopolitan,* August 2008, p. 39.

Chapter 5. Found in Translation

1. Brandon Hurst, *Scarlett Johansson* (London: A Jot Publishing, Ltd., 2009), p. 45.

2. Reviews of *An American Rhapsody,* directed by Éva Gárdos, *Rotten Tomatoes,* n.d., <http://www.rottentomatoes. com/m/american_rhapsody/?page=2&critic=columns&sortby= date&name_order=asc&view=#contentReviews> (December 1, 2009).

3. Ibid.

4. Frank Lovece, review of *An American Rhapsody,* directed by Éva Gárdos, *TV Guide,* n.d., <http://movies.tvguide.com/american-rhapsody/review/135362> (December 1, 2009).

5. "An American Rhapsody," *Box Office Mojo,* n.d., <http://boxofficemojo.com/movies/?id=americanrhapsody.htm> (December 1, 2009).

6. Ibid.

7. Alicia Clott, "Spotlight on Scarlett Johansson," *Girls' Life,* June/July 2002, <http://www.thefreelibrary.com/Scarlett+Johansson.+(Spotlight).-a086705229> (August 23, 2010).

8. Ibid.

9. Ibid.

10. Stephen Hunter, "'Freaks': This Tickling Monster Flick Has Got Legs," *Washington Post,* July 17, 2002, <http://www.washingtonpost.com/ac2/wp-dyn?pagename=article&node=&contentId=A16290-2002Jul16&notFound=true> (December 2, 2009).

11. Clott.

12. David Ansen and Devin Gordon, "Scarlett Fever," *Newsweek,* September 22, 2003, <http://www.newsweek.com/2003/09/14/scarlett-fever.html> (August 23, 2010).

13. Graham Fuller, "Scarlett Johansson," *Interview,* September 2003, <http://www.ebscohost.com/> (December 5, 2009).

14. Pippa Smith, "Scarlett: The Truth About My Threesome," *Independent,* August 16, 2008, <http://www.independent.ie/entertainment/film-cinema/scarlett-the-truth-about-my-threesome-1456865.html> (October 13, 2009).

15. Polly Vernon, "Scarlett Fever," *London Guardian,* December 28, 2003, <http://www.guardian.co.uk/film/2003/dec/28/features.magazine> (November 17, 2009).

16.Karen S. Schneider, Rebecca Paley, and Alison Singh Gee, "Real Attitude," *People,* October 6, 2003, <http://www.

people.com/people/archive/article/00,20148275,00.html> (August 23, 2010).

17. Ibid.

18. Reviews of *Lost in Translation,* directed by Sofia Coppola, *Rotten Tomatoes,* n.d., <http://www.rottentomatoes. com/m/lost_in_translation/> (December 5, 2009).

19. David Ansen and Devin Gordon, "Scarlett Fever," *Newsweek,* September 22, 2003, <http://www.newsweek. com/2003/09/14/scarlett-fever.html> (August 23, 2010).

20. Eleanor Ringel Gillespie, review of *Lost in Translation,* directed by Sofia Coppola, *accessAtlanta,* n.d., <http://www. accessatlanta.com/movies/content/shared/movies/reviews/L/los-tintranslation.html> (December 7, 2009).

21. Personal interview with James Berardinelli, January 27, 2010.

22. Ibid.

23. Ibid.

24. Tania Shakinovsky and Nicole Lampert, "Scarlett, the Movie Queen," *London Evening Standard,* February 16, 2004, <http://www.thisislondon.co.uk/film/article-9165453-scarlett-the-movie-queen.do> (November 25, 2009).

25. David Gritten, Tim Robey, and Sukhdev Sandhu, "The Films That Defined the Noughties," *London Telegraph,* November 6, 2009, <http://www.telegraph.co.uk/culture/film/6501160/Top-100-movies-defining-the-noughties-00s-in-film.html> (December 4, 2009).

Chapter 6. The Queen of Independents

1. Personal interview with James Berardinelli, January 27, 2010.

2. Kate Meyers, "Scarlett in Wonderland," *InStyle,* October 2006, <http://www.ebscohost.com/> (October 12, 2009).

3. Ibid.

4. Ibid.

5. Tom Sykes, "Scarlett Johansson's Sexy Style," *Harper's*

Bazaar, January 2005, <http://www.ebscohost.com/> (October 12, 2009).

6. "First Lady of Film: Scarlett Johansson," *Cosmopolitan,* December 2006, <http://www.ebscohost.com/> (October 12, 2009).

7. Ibid.

8. Melena Ryzik, "Local Favourite," *Sydney Morning Herald,* September 17, 2007, <http://www.smh.com.au/ news/film/local-favourite/2007/09/16/1189881329353.html> (October 13, 2009).

9. Ibid.

10. Meyers.

11. "Johansson Disgusted With Hollywood Attitude to Weight," *TeenHollywood.com,* September 15, 2006, <http:// www.teenhollywood.com/2006/09/15/johannson-disgusted-with-hollywood-attitude-to-weight> (October 13, 2009).

12. Sykes.

13. *TeenHollywood.com.*

14. Sykes.

15. Richard Roeper, review of *Girl With a Pearl Earring,* directed by Peter Webber, *Rotten Tomatoes,* n.d., <http://www. rottentomatoes.com/m/girl_with_a_pearl_earring/?critic=cream crop#contentReviews> (September 9, 2010).

16. Keith Dovkants, "Scarlett's Journey to the Top," *London Evening Standard,* February 18, 2004, <http://www. thisislondon.co.uk/film/article-9210050-scarletts-journey-to-the-top.do> (November 25, 2009).

17. Review of *Girl With a Pearl Earring,* directed by Peter Webber, *Rotten Tomatoes,* n.d., <http://www.rottentomatoes. com/m/girl_with_a_pearl_earring/?critic=columns&sortby= name&name_order=asc&view=#contentReviews> (November 25, 2009).

18. "Girl With a Pearl Earring," *Box Office Mojo,* n.d., <http://boxofficemojo.com/movies/?id=girlwithapearlearring. htm> (November 25, 2009).

19. Mick LaSalle, "Film Clips: The Perfect Score," *San*

Francisco Examiner, January 30, 2004, <http://www.sfgate. com/cgi-bin/article.cgi?f=/c/a/2004/01/30/DDGKP4KA531. DTL> (December 17, 2009).

20. Scott Weinberg, review of *The Perfect Score,* directed by Brian Robbins, *eFilmCritic,* February 14, 2004, <http://efilm-critic.com/review.php?movie=8628&reviewer=128> (December 17, 2009).

21. "Scarlett Johansson—Johansson: Americans 'Disappointed' by Bush's Re-election," *Contactmusic.com,* August 23, 2005, <http://www.contactmusic.com/new/ xmlfeed.nsf/story/johansson-americans-disappointed-by-bushs-re-election> (December 21, 2009).

22. Polly Vernon, "Scarlett Fever," *London Guardian,* December 28, 2003, <http://www.guardian.co.uk/film/2003/ dec/28/features.magazine> (November 17, 2009).

23. Brandon Hurst, *Scarlett Johansson* (London: A Jot Publishing, Ltd., 2009), p. 100.

24. Ibid.

25. Chris Roberts, *Scarlett Johansson: Portrait of a Rising Star* (London: Carlton Books, 2007), p. 71.

26. "The SpongeBob SquarePants Movie," *Box Office Mojo,* n.d., <http://boxofficemojo.com/movies/?id=spongebob. htm> (December 23, 2009).

27. David Ansen, "In Good Company: Even Now, Father Knows Best," *Newsweek,* December 20, 2004, *msnbc. com,* 2010, <http://msnbc.msn.com/id/6699970/site/news-week/38376722> (September 7, 2010).

28. "In Good Company," *Box Office Mojo,* n.d., <http:// boxofficemojo.com/movies/?id=ingoodcompany.htm> (December 23, 2009).

29. Claudia Puig, "'Woman,' Thy Film Is Not All Good," *USA Today,* February 2, 2006, <http://www.usatoday.com/life/ movies/reviews/2006-02-02-good-woman_x.htm> (December 23, 2009).

30. "A Love Song for Bobby Long," *Box Office Mojo,*

n.d., <http://boxofficemojo.commovies/?id= lovesongforbobbylong.htm> (December 23, 2009).

··

Chapter 7. Woody's Muse?

1. Liza Foreman, "Johansson Onboard Allen Film," *Hollywood Reporter,* June 29, 2004, *AllBusiness.com,* 2010, <http://www.allbusiness.com/services/motion-pic-tures/4888698-1.html> (August 23, 2010).

2. Brandon Hurst, *Scarlett Johansson* (London: A Jot Publishing, Ltd., 2009), p. 103.

3. Jeffrey Stinson, "Hollywood Enters the Era of Scarlett Johansson," *USA Today,* August 21, 2007, <http://www. usatoday.com/life/movies/news/2007-08-21-scarlett-johansson-cover_N.htm> (October 13, 2009).

4. "Woody Allen 'Scarlett Johansson Touched by God,'" *Female First,* n.d., <http://www.femalefirst.co.uk/celebrity/ Scarlett+Johansson-518.html> (December 29, 2009).

5. Mick Martin and Marsha Porter, *DVD and Video Guide 2007* (New York: Ballantine Books, 2006), p. 720.

6. Bill Muller, review of *Match Point,* directed by Woody Allen, *Arizona Republic,* January 20, 2006, <http://www. azcentral.com/ent/movies/articles/0120matchpoint0120.html> (December 29, 2009).

7. John Travolta, "Scarlett Johansson," *Interview,* November 2005, <http://www.ebscohost.com/> (October 28, 2009).

8. Paul Clinton, "Review: Woody Allen Back on His Game," *CNN.com,* January 6, 2006, <http://www.cnn. com/2006/SHOWBIZ/Movies/01/06/review.match/index. html> (December 29, 2009).

9. "Match Point," *Box Office Mojo,* n.d., <http://boxof-ficemojo.com/movies/?id=matchpoint.htm> (December 29, 2009).

10. Ibid.

11. Brian D. Johnson, "Woody, Women and Nymphs," *Maclean's,* January 16, 2006, <http://www.

macleans.ca/culture/entertainment/article.jsp?id=0&conte
nt=20060116_119692_119692> (September 7, 2010).

12. Ibid.

13. Stinson,

14. Kenneth Whyte, "Interview With Woody Allen," *Maclean's,* January 3, 2008, <http://www.macleans.ca/homep-age/magazine/article.jsp?content=20080103_113117_5196> (Septembe 7, 2010).

15. "Scoop," *Box Office Mojo,* n.d., <http://boxofficemojo.com/movies/?id=scoop.htm> (December 30, 2009).

16. Alex Sandell, review of *Scoop,* directed by Woody Allen, *Juicy Cerebellum,* n.d., <http://www.juicycerebellum.com/200616.htm> (December 30, 2009).

17. Ibid.

18. Denise Wild, "Scarlett Johansson," *Tribute,* October 2008, <http://www.ebscohost.com/> (October 12, 2009).

19. "First Lady of Film: Scarlett Johansson," *Cosmopolitan,* December 2006, <http://www.ebscohost.com/> (October 12, 2009).

20. John Hiscock, "Treasure Island," *London Daily Mirror,* December 8, 2005, <http://www.mirror.co.uk/tv-entertainment/ archive/interviews/2005/08/12/treasure-island-115875-15841157/> (January 4, 2010).

21. "The Black Dahlia," *Box Office Mojo,* n.d., <http://boxofficemojo.com/movies/?id=blackdahlia.htm> (January 4, 2010).

22. "The Prestige," *Box Office Mojo,* n.d., <http://box offic-emojo.com/movies/?id=prestige.htm> (January 6, 2010).

23. James Inverne, "Lloyd Webber Wants Scarlett Johansson for London *Sound of Music,*" *Playbill,* May 9, 2005, <http://www.playbill.com/news/article/92834-Lloyd-Webber-Wants-Scarlett-Johansson-for-London-Sound-of-Music> (January 7, 2010).

24. "Johansson Snubs *Sound of Music,*" *Contactmusic.com,* July 27, 2006, <http://www.contactmusic.com/news.nsf/story/johansson-snubs-sound-of-music_1003667> (January 7, 2010).

25. Ibid.

Chapter 8. Actor and Altruist

1. John Hiscock, "Treasure Island," *London Daily Mirror,* December 8, 2005, <http://www.mirror.co.uk/ tv-entertainment/archive/interviews/2005/08/12/treasure-island-115875-15841157/> (January 4, 2010).

2. WENN.com, "Hartnett Opens Up About 'Painful' Johansson Split," *Hollywood.com,* January 31, 2007, <http:// www.hollywood.com/news/Hartnett_Opens_Up_About_ Painful_Johansson_Split/3651200> (October 13, 2009).

3. Ibid.

4. Brandon Hurst, *Scarlett Johansson* (London: A Jot Publishing, Ltd., 2009), pp. 158–159.

5. Amiel Martin Cabanlig, "Compassion," *Manila Times,* March 8, 2008, <http://archives.manilatimes.net/nation-al/2008/mar/08/yehey/life/20080308lif1.html> (September 7, 2010).

6. Sheryl Garratt, "The Jewel of India: Scarlett Johansson," *London Daily Mail,* June 18, 2007, <http://www.dailymail. co.uk/home/you/article-462179/The-jewel-India-Scarlett-Johansson.html> (October 26, 2009).

7. Ibid.

8. Ibid.

9. Gina Shaw, "Scarlett Johansson Feeds Hungry Children," *WebMD,* October 28, 2009, <http://children. webmd.com/features/scarlett-johansson-feeds-hungry-children?print=true#> (November 24, 2009).

10. Ibid.

11. Ibid.

12. John Wirt, "Ill-defined Characters Spoil 'Nanny Diaries,'" *Baton Rouge Advocate,* n.d., <http:// www.2theadvocate.com/entertainment/movies/reviews/ 9476657.html> (January 15, 2010).

13. Sean O'Connell, review of *The Nanny Diaries,* directed by Robert Pulcini and Shari Springer Berman, *Filmcritic.com,*

August 4, 2006, <http://www.filmcritic.com/misc/emporium. nsf/reviews/The-Nanny-Diaries> (January 11, 2010).

14. Rebecca Winters Keegan, "Red-Hot Scarlett," *Cosmopolitan,* August 2008, p. 40.

15. Stephen Mooallem, "Scarlett Johansson," *Interview,* June/July 2008, <http://www.interviewmagazine.com/music/ scarlett-johansson/> (August 23, 2010).

16. Chris Willman, "The Best and Worst of 2008," *EW.com,* n.d., <http://www.ew.com/ew/gallery/0,,20162677_ 20164091_20247309_14,00.html> (January 11, 2010).

17. Priya Elan, "Scarlett Johansson: *Anywhere I Lay My Head,*" *NME.com,* May 2, 2008, <http://www.nme.com/ reviews/scarlett-johansson/9660> (August 23, 2010).

18. "The Other Boleyn Girl," *Box Office Mojo,* n.d., <http://boxofficemojo.com/movies/?id=otherboleyngirl.htm> (January 11, 2010).

19. Roger Ebert, review of *Vicky Cristina Barcelona,* directed by Woody Allen, *RogerEbert.com,* August 14, 2008, <http:// rogerebert.suntimes.com/apps/pbcs.dll/article?AID=/20080814/ REVIEWS/808140305/1023> (January 11, 2010).

20. Stephen Ostermiller, "Pound Sterling (GPB) Currency Exchange Rate Conversion Calculator," *CoinMill.com,* 2010, <http://coinmill.com/GBP_calculator.html#GBP=20> (January 11, 2010).

21. "Fan Pays 20,000 Pounds to Date Scarlett," *BBC News,* March 14, 2008, <http://news.bbc.co.uk/2/hi/ entertainment/7295871.stm> (October 13, 2009).

22. "Biography for Scarlett Johansson," *IMDB.com,* n.d., <http://www.imdb.com/name/nm0424060/> (November 25, 2009).

23. Sarah Cristobel, "Scarlett Center Stage," *Harpers Bazaar,* February 2009, <http://www.harpersbazaar.com/ magazine/cover/scarlett-johansson-cover-story-0209> (November 24, 2009).

24. Personal interview with James Berardinelli, January 27, 2010.

25. Ibid.

26. James Robinson, "Scarlett Johansson Threatens to Sue *Cosmopolitan* in Dispute Over Quotes," *London Guardian,* December 16, 2008, <http://www.guardian.co.uk/media/2008/dec/15/scarlett-johansson-threatens-cosmopolitan-lawsuit> (December 16, 2008).

27. James Robinson, "*Cosmopolitan* Says Sorry to Scarlett Johansson for Disputed Quotes," *London Guardian,* December 19, 2008,<http://www.guardian.co.uk/media/2008/dec/19/cosmopolitan-apologises-to-scarlett-johansson> (December 23, 2008).

28. "He's Just Not That Into You," *Box Office Mojo,* n.d., <http://www.boxofficemojo.com/movies/?id=hesjustnotthatintoyou.htm> (January 11, 2010).

29. Mick LaSalle, review of *He's Just Not That Into You,* directed by Ken Kwapis, *San Francisco Chronicle,* February 6, 2009, <http://www.sfgate.com/cgi-bin/article.cgi?f=/c/a/2009/02/05/DDHM15N9QF.DTL&type=movies> (January 12, 2010).

30. Leah Greenblatt, "Music Review: *Break Up* (2009)," *EW.com,* September 2, 2009, <http://www.ew.com/ew/article/0,,20302008,00.html> (January 12, 2010).

31. "Scarlett Johansson's New Year's Pizza," *Monsters and Critics,* December 29, 2009, <http://www.monstersandcritics.com/people/news/article_1521901.php/Scarlett-Johansson-s-New-Year-s-pizza> (September 8, 2010).

32. Patrick Healy, "'Red and Memphis' Win Top Tony Awards," *New York Times,* June 13, 2010, <http://www.nytimes.com/2010/06/14/theater/theaterspecial/14tony.html?hp> (November 2, 2010).

33. Scott Huver, "How Scarlett Johansson Shaped Up for *Iron Man 2,*" *People,* July 27, 2009, <http://www.people.com/people/article/0,,20293953,00.html> (November 3, 2010).

FURTHER READING

Belli, Mary Lou, and Dinah Lenney. *Acting for Young Actors: The Ultimate Teen Guide.* New York: Backstage Books, 2006.

Connolly, Sean. *Oxfam.* Collingwood, Ontario: Saunders Book Company, 2009.

Hurst, Brandon. *Scarlett Johansson.* London, U.K.: A Jot, 2007.

Roberts, Chris. *Scarlett Johansson: Portrait of a Rising Star.* Bishopbriggs, Glasgow, U.K.: Carlton Books, Ltd., 2007.

INTERNET ADDRESSES

Scarlett Johansson, *People Magazine*
http://www.people.com/people/scarlett_johansson

Scarlett Johansson, *Yahoo! Movies*
http://movies.yahoo.com/movie/contributor/1800022348/bio

Oxfam International
http://www.oxfam.org/

INDEX